Danilo Attardi

Fashion Moulage Techn

Fashion Moulage Techn

Danilo Attardi

Danilo Attardi is a fashion designer for women, men and children, a dressmaker and creator of models; he owns a fashion design studio and works as a consultant for several companies in the sector. During his first year of study he participated in international events at AltaRoma. After training in Rome, Milan and Florence, he set up his own company, Danilo Attardi Studio. Since 2008 he has been designing and developing the Danilo Attardi and ADverso women's clothing lines. He has also styled major personalities from the world of Italian show business. For years he has been organising courses in style and design, dedicating himself with passion to the training of professionals and students of fashion design and draping in Europe and the United States.

www.daniloattardi.it

Fashion Moulage Technique

A Step by Step Draping Course

Dresses
Collars
Drapes
Knots
Volumes
Sleeves

PROMOPRESS 11

Fashion Moulage Technique
A Step by Step Draping Course

Original title:
La tecnica del moulage

English translation by Mariotti
Translations

ISBN: 978-84-17412-12-8
D.L.: B 28000-2018

Promopress is a brand of:
Promotora de prensa internacional S.A.
C/ Ausiàs March 124
08013 Barcelona, Spain
Tel.: 0034 93 245 14 64
Fax: 0034 93 265 48 83
Email: info@promopress.es
www.promopresseditions.com
Facebook: Promopress Editions
Twitter: Promopress Editions @
PromopressEd

First published in English: 2019

The photos accompanying the text of the
manual are the property of the author.
For the photos in the introduction:
ASA Milano, pages 8 and 9.
Federico Garolla, page 10.
Indigitalimages, pages 11, 12 and 13

Editing: Martina Panarello
Layout: spread
Cover design: spread

Printed in Turkey

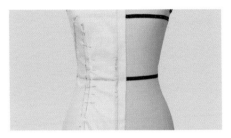

Contents

Introduction

Sculpture of Artemis,
Pergamonmuseum, Berlin.

Moulage, also known as Draping, is a technique that allows you to create an item of clothing directly on the dress stand. Used in Haute Couture, it has always existed, even before modelling. The term is of French origin and means "cast" or "mould", and this is what we will be doing, sculpting the toile on our dress stand.

Imagination and freedom are the key principles of Moulage. In fact, based on three-dimensionality, it allows the creation of original garments, from classic draping to more articulated and structured designs. Step by step the model will take shape on the dress stand, from the sketch directly to the fabric.

Fashion always needs to reinvent itself, but in this continuous evolution, design remains a fixed point. Working with Moulage has allowed every designer-modeller to materialise their vision. With the model created directly on the dress stand we can manage style and fit at any time. The results will be new models, cuts and lines that will give life to a new three-dimensional prototype, without the standardised impositions of modelling.

The model is not built from a flat 2D figure, but from three-dimensionality. This allows the designer to have an early idea of their creation and to decide how to move forward. All of this through the use of a toile, pins, pleats, craftsmanship, modules, draping, and a lot of creativity.

Moulage is not just draping, but a technique that allows us to find solutions where modelling has not succeeded. However, I would like to point out that it does not replace modelling: the two techniques work and interact together.

Before the arrival of the modelling, one worked directly on the customer or on the dress stand. The need to

charge of the wardrobe who took great care over every fold of the fabric. This operation was done on wooden trestles, the precursors of modern dress stands.

The different ways of draping the fabric have marked the various Greco-Roman eras, but, generally, the models were simple and not very original, enriched with jewels, ornaments and, in the case of women, sophisticated hairstyles.

The invention of the first models of cut and stitched clothes dates back to the Middle Ages and the appearance of the first tailor's shops. Having abandoned the draping of Roman costumes, a fashion spread throughout the West that was just as simple but characterised by more adherent lines designed to emphasise the shape of the body. The women's tunic, in particular, hugged the bust and then fell smoothly down to the feet. From this point on begins the fashion of flared and very wide sleeves that characterised the entire Middle Ages.

In the period of the Seignories, between the 12th and 14th centuries, there was a marked improvement in economic conditions. Luxury and richness become the key words for the making of clothes: damasks, silks, velvets and embroideries embellish the garments, which now, more than ever, are a symbol of social status. The use of these fabrics coincides with the invention and improvement of looms and weaving machines, which are now more sophisticated and able to create different shapes. The models worn by the ladies are slinky, but the sleeve is the richest and most important part of the dress, which was often adorned with precious metals, gems and buttons.

Following the Middle Ages, the Renaissance, which from Italy spread throughout Europe, gave women's

start working with paper patterns coincided with the need to meet the demand of large retailers and prêt-à-porter: a fast method that would satisfy the demand of mass consumption.

This technique helps the designer to find new ideas, the pattern maker to complete a precise and fast piece of work (ensuring a result when this cannot be achieved with a dress pattern), the seamstress to make her clothes to measure, and the young student or fashion enthusiast to see their own Capsule Collection realised.

The origins of this way of creating clothes can be traced back to Ancient Greece. Women and men, in fact, wore unstitched, highly draped, unstructured clothes, closed at the waist and shoulders with belts and buckles, thus giving rise to a Moulage that we could call "primitive", as represented by the peplos and the chiton.

So Greek clothing becomes a symbol of how culture can also influence aspects of everyday life, such as fashion. Indeed,the value of freedom was for the ancient Greeks a cornerstone of their way of acting and thinking, and their clothes perfectly reflect this principle: the body had to be free from all constraint. Their robes were, therefore, soft, allowing the body freedom of movement, and were made of a raw wool fabric, later replaced by finer materials and, finally, linen.

This characteristic fluid line was then taken up by the Romans, who considered stitched clothes a feature of barbarian peoples. The toga, the most representative garment of the Roman age, was a semicircular cloak made of wool cloth which was wrapped around the body without seams. Made in different colours depending on social status or special public duties, the toga was prepared, before being worn, by the slaves in

Roberto Capucci, AW 1953.

clothing fuller forms, expanding the line of the hips and emphasising the procacity of the breast. Model books with drawings and sketches began to spread; modelling became increasingly refined, and tailors used these books both as samples for customers and as a source of inspiration for the creation of new cuts.

In the baroque era the line of the clothes becomes curved, and skirts become wider and more flamboyant. Wigs and bows, flowers and ribbons enrich the dresses of the ladies at the court of Versailles, where everything is luxurious and sparkling. This helps to establish the close link that Paris and fashion will have in the centuries to come.

Between the end of the 17th century and the beginning of the 18th spread the use of panniers, rigid hoops almost always made of rush which, positioned around the hips, extended the width of the skirt. A constant presence in women's clothing is the bust, which over the centuries has altered its shape and texture, and it is in the 18th century that a more comfortable and less rigid model is invented, composed of thin, flexible splints. It will take several more years before women are freed from this bodily constraint in favour of the enhancement of their body with the use of special cuts and models.

All studies of costume and fashion attribute to Charles Frederick Worth (1825-1895), the tailor-couturier, the merit of having revolutionised the way of making and creating clothes. His was the first real "fashion house", where the choice of outfit was no longer entirely up to the customer, who now was merely allowed to choose between the various models, styles and fabrics presented by Worth. The tailor was no longer considered a simple craftsman, but

silhouette gradually changed and, from 1910, the empire line prevailed in their clothes. In these years the models changed quickly: significant was the transition from an A-line, with a thin waist and a wide skirt, to a smoother, more flowing line, perfectly represented by the Delphos dress pioneered by Mariano Fortuny in 1907.

These were the years when Paris was the capital of European fashion, where the names of those designers who were destined to change the rules of clothing forever dominated: Lanvin, Chanel, Patou, Vionnet, Molyneux.

Active in the cultural debate on women's clothing in the early 1900s, Madeleine Vionnet (1876-1975) opened her first workshop in Paris in 1912. The careful study of the elasticity of the fabrics and patterns worn in the classical age, allow her to banish seams and model the fabric directly on the body. Madame Vionnet experiments with the Moulage technique on a small dress stand, creating simple and elegant models, where any superfluous decoration is banned. The renewed neoclassical taste of those years and the introduction of her innovative way of cutting clothes on the bias ensure her success as a

became a real artist, no longer able to just accommodate the tastes of the ladies, but to propose his ideas, thus creating a personal style. Worth was the first to sign his own creations, giving rise to Haute Couture. With the opening of his shop in rue de la Pax 7 in Paris, the first Maison was born and, with it, the first "fashion shows" for customers.

Already by the middle of the 19th century, the first feminist movements for the recognition of women's full rights began to appear, but it was only in the 20th century that the long and difficult road to women's emancipation and universal suffrage attained its first results. With the men away fighting in the trenches during the Great War, many women left the home to work. Their role in society changed and, with it, so did fashion. Throughout Europe the need to abolish the slavery of the bust arose, the female

Balenciaga SS 2017.

designer, with many of her creations being worn movie stars.

In the same years, Madame Grès reinvents the technique of draping: a master in modelling the canvas, creator of apparently simple models but with a complex soul, she worked in three dimensions, composing the draping around a real body. Madame Grès sculpts the fabric creating relief elements, ruches and plissé, beautiful but also functional dresses, in which women were still free to move.

Then we have Dior who, through Moulage, succeeds in sculpting his idea of woman on the dress stand, giving life to his collections. The fashion show that brought him success was the one presented on February 12, 1947, in his historic headquarters at 30 Avenue Montaigne, which had two leitmotifs: "En huit" and "Corolle". "It's a New Look," exclaimed Carmel Snow, editor of Harper's Bazaar: it was immediately a revolution. The piece that still represents and keeps alive those years of the house of Dior is the Tailleur Bar.

After the Second World War, many couturiers resumed their activities. One of the most famous was the House of Chanel, where hats, accessories and later clothes take shape thanks to Moulage. The use of jersey and experimenting with the three-piece dress, composed of a short, straight skirt, a sweater and a jacket-cardigan, make the house and its founder icons of elegance.

At the same time Paris sees the opening of a boutique by newly-arrived Elsa Schiaparelli, one of the most famous Italian designers who gave fashion an extravagant, almost surrealist impulse. Eclectic and nonconformist, Elsa is one of the first to study her collections on the basis of a single theme, creating whimsical clothes and accessories. The style she created is a play of shapes, colours and almost dreamlike designs: lobsters, elephants, giant mouths, mirrors. But there is no lack of rigour and accuracy in the execution of her clothes.

In Italy, in the 50s, Capucci with great skill invents original shapes and volumes, ruches and plissé.

And Cristobal Balenciaga, albeit in a more modern key, revolutionises the female silhouette, freeing it from structures and bodices by eliminating the waistline. Architect of fashion, master of cutting and precision, thanks to his ideas that took shape with Moulage, he gave us the tunic dress, the sack dress, pinafores and bubble skirts. Balenciaga immediately understood the importance of the fabric, a fundamental element for the final result, and invented Gazar, a fabric usually made of silk or wool with a simple weave, but with a special characteristic: its particular stiff consistency held the shape modelled

Zack Posen AW 2013-14.

Iris Van Herpen SS 2017.

Maison Margiela AW 2015-16.

on the dress stand, allowing the fabric's full potential to be discovered and new, never before attempted, forms to be created.

In the 90s it was the turn of the French and Japanese avant-garde: Issey Miyake, Margiela, Comme de Garçons, Thierry Mugler, Yohji Yamamoto and many others.

Many Designer-Couturiers who use Moulage believe that it is an essential tool for managing every stage of the creation and production process.

Still today, many designers use this technique; the names of the great historic French houses are joined by the post-contemporary vision of the new northern European talents: Gareth Pugh, Iris Van Herpen, Haider Ackermann, and maybe you'll be next.

Moulage may replace the blank sheet, but remember that behind every creation there is always a good idea. Whatever the number of models to be created, the model has to be studied and, just as every architect

formulates a project, every garment must be conceived in the same way: it should be beautiful, new, comfortable, functional, and of quality.

The beauty of Moulage is that there are no limits! The only barrier is your creativity.

Work
tools

Dress stands

The world of dress stands is infinite. There are a number of international manufacturers including Siegel-Stockman, Tailor'S and Bonaveri.

Whatever the brand, a good dress stand must have a rigid polyurethane interior and must be covered with fabric to allow pinning.

Tailor's dummies for display are also available, whose interior is made of polystyrene. I do not recommend the latter, as they almost never respect proportions and can easily become deformed, meaning they lack the accuracy needed for a perfect job.

Sizes vary depending on the manufacturer: make a targeted choice and buy a dress stand that comes as close as possible to your size chart and your needs, because, although here we are talking about a size 42, even within the same company (as in the case of Stockman) there can be different types of dress stands with different sizes, depending on whether it is an Haute Couture, Pret a Porter or Atelier mannequin.

The best choice would be to have one produced with your own size chart as reference.

There is a wide range of useful accessories for making any item of clothing: depending on your requirements, you can buy arms, legs, a head, etc.

In addition, adjustable dress stands are also available, useful for made-to-measure garments. The ideal would be to have a number of dress stands of different sizes and then to buy an adjustable one, if necessary, useful for made-to-measure and to check for any changes in the size.

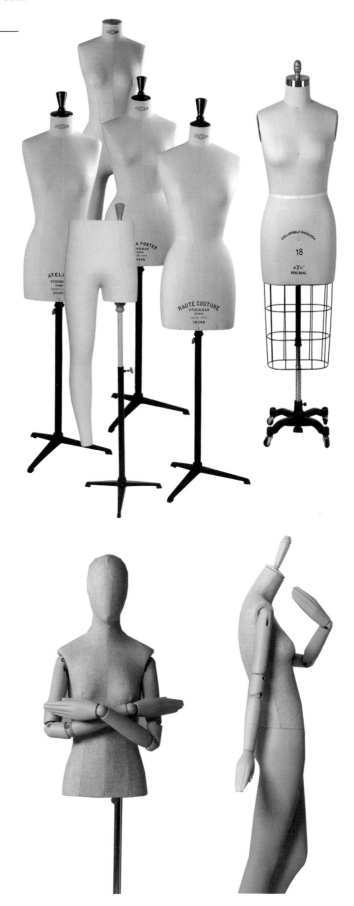

Toile fabric

Plain weave

Plain weave fabric is a thin, flat and flexible surface, consisting of a crossing and assembly of fibres of different kinds known as weave. There are different types of fabric on the market, but as far as we are concerned we will only talk about those suitable for making models, with a basic plain weave.

The toile is a simple weave of warp (vertical threads parallel to the selvedge) and weft (horizontal threads running from selvedge to selvedge).

The toile used must have characteristics as similar as possible to those of the fabric chosen to make the garment.

Handle the fabric gently, without forcing it too much, otherwise it could yield and fail. You should move it as naturally as possible.

Cotton toile should be no more than 1.50 m (59.05") high, since fabrics usually do not exceed 1.20-1.50 m (47.24-59.05") in clothing.

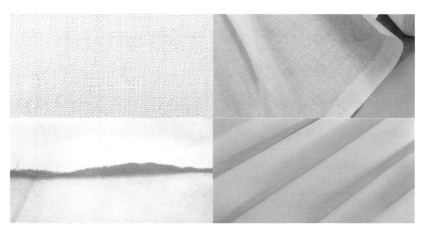

Different types of toile.

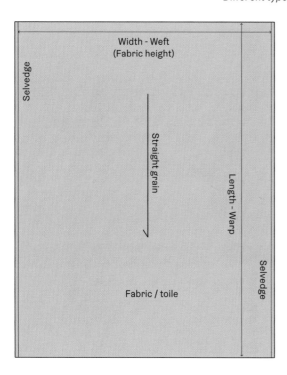

Working on the straight grain

The toile has its own structure, so if positioned and worked on the straight grain it becomes stiff and does not move, but if moved in other directions, such as the bias, the fabric becomes soft, flowing and comfortable.

The secret of Moulage lies in learning how to handle the fabric, trying to move and model it in harmony with its structure. Let the fabric itself guide you and learn how to feel its movement. There are no mathematical rules, but with passion, commitment and the exercises in this book you will soon come up with new and original solutions.

Working on the bias

The bias is the 45° axis between the warp and weft of the toile: it is used for different types of clothes since working on the straight grain does not always produce the desired effects. Working with the fabric on the bias almost always results in a consumption equal to twice the area to be worked.

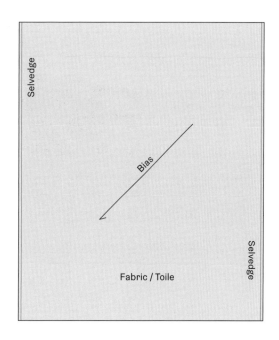

The elasticity of the Bias
By pulling the two opposite corners of a fabric, i.e. the bias, we can see that it stretches as if it were elasticated.

Just think of the petticoat type baby-doll dress: being cut on the bias, it can also be worn without any opening (zip, buttons).

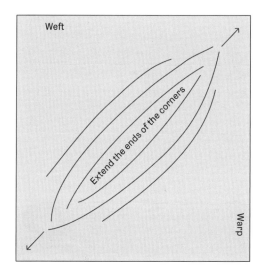

Softness of the Bias
The image on the right shows the movement of the fabric on the bias if we took the corner of the toile at the intersection of the warp and weft: in this way, thanks to the force of gravity, numerous pleats are created, similar to rays of sunshine, to give an effect of softness.

This example helps us to understand how to position the fabric on the dress stand to create different and infinite drapings.

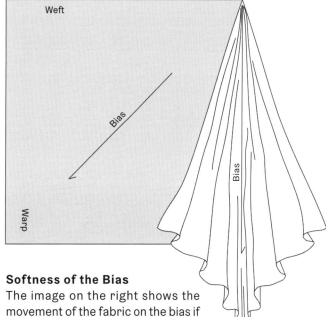

Other tools

Toile, pins, webbing, adhesive tape, scissors, rulers, set squares, French curves, pencils, and coloured pens are indispensable tools for working properly with this technique.

We will use a lot of pins, so I would recommend buying buy a box of at least 250 g.

And don't forget a needlework table and a steam iron.

I have listed only the tools we are going to use the most, but in a design and tailoring studio there is this and much more.

5 mm wide webbing/tape/Drittofilo cotton ribbon (colour contrasting with the dress stand).

Long, thin pins. Do not use ones with plastic heads.

Set squares, rulers and French curves.

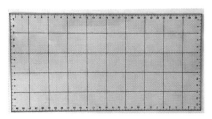

Tape measure, adhesive tape and scissors.

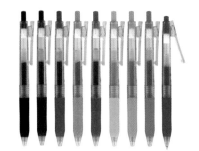

Coloured pens, iron and notch pliers.

How to detect and mark the principal points on the dress stand

To start working with the Moulage-Draping technique and construct a model directly on the dress stand, you must first mark the principal control points. Further asymmetrical cuts, necklines or special features of the model can be marked later.

We will use 0.5 cm (0.19") high cotton webbing (Drittofilo ribbon), the colour of which should be in contrast with the dress stand so we can clearly see the principal lines. So, we will put black webbing on a white dress stand, and white webbing on a black dress stand.

Begin by marking the Centre front and then the Centre back. The webbing must be placed exactly on the vertical axis of the Centre front: start from the top, i.e. the middle of the neck and use a pin to secure the webbing. The pin must pass through the tape going from top to bottom, following the line of the tape, and its point must remain inside.

Now secure the end of the webbing; here I suggest you place the pin horizontally, because if you put it vertically the point would come out and you could injure yourself.

After ensuring that the webbing is exactly in line with the vertical axis and that the dress stand is visually divided into two, attach the other pins. They must be positioned in the same way, spaced a maximum of 2 cm (0.78") apart. The more pins the better, because one must keep in mind that later on we will have to work and model the toile on the dress stand, so the tape should be secured as firmly as possible. Repeat these steps to mark the Center back.

For the principal levels, position the webbing at bust level (at the fullest point), waist level (on the narrowest point) and hip level (on the widest point), exactly in line with the horizontal axis. The pins will now be positioned in the direction of the webbing, i.e. no longer from top to bottom, but from right to left (or from left to right if you are left-handed).

Continue through the neck, shoulder, armholes and side line. The pins should always be attached along the line of the webbing, keeping the point inside.

It is important to note that the lines shown on the dress stand are only references, which should accurately reflect our size charts. In addition, with regard to the position of the side reference line, if in modelling we are accustomed to having the front 2 cm (0.78") larger than the back, then this will be borne in mind.

So, depending on the type of model chosen, the seams of the shoulder or side, the armholes and any asymmetrical cuts may therefore not align with the lines initially shown on the dress stand.

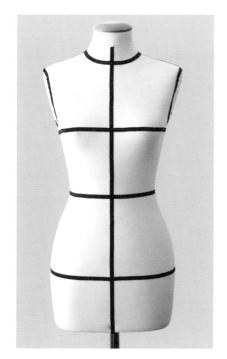
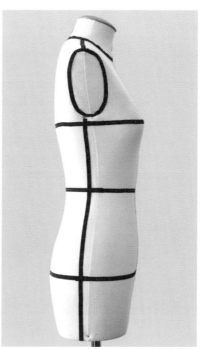
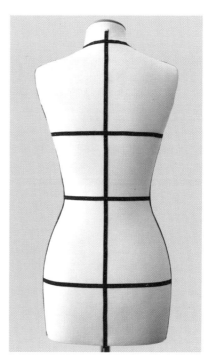

Practical advice

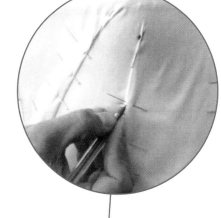

The pins should always be positioned perpendicular to the cut: in this way the model will dress better where there are curves and then it will be easier to properly mark the seams (1).

Darts should be marked entirely with dotted lines at close intervals. Since the dart always shrinks away, mark a point at the height of its tip, precisely 1 cm (0.39") before it ends. (2).

Seams or cuts should be marked from start to finish entirely with dotted lines at close intervals (3).

In a complex model with several seams or cuts, use different colours to mark them, and in the centre of each add a notch with an identification letter or number. The notch will always be of a different colour to the dotted lines and this will help to reassemble the pieces.

The pleats should be marked with dotted lines only for the first 3-4 cm (1.18-1.57"), the direction set and, if there are several pleats, mark them with different colours and number them (4).

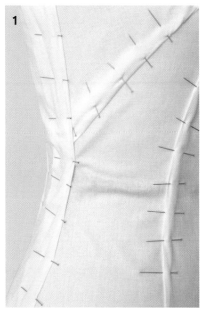

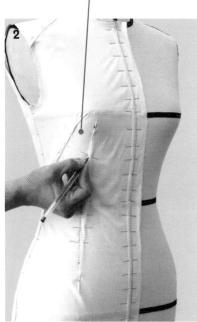

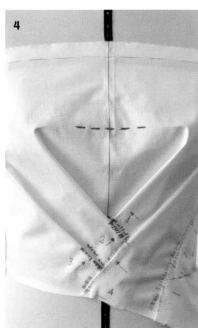

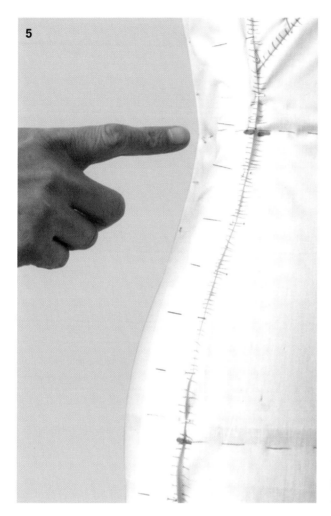

Mark all control points with a dotted line at waist level, hip level, and bust level (5), and if there are seam movements that do not align with the standard control points, such as the shoulder seam moving forward as if it were a yoke, still mark the shoulder line control point on the toile.

For collars or volumes, the pins should be positioned along the seam otherwise, if placed perpendicularly, they could create problems with the toile (6).

The decisive cut

Another action that will help to solve a whole series of problems related to the rigidity of the straight grain fabric, the modelling of collars, basques or volumes, the creation of a knot or an entire garment that looks like a rose, is a cut. This is because, as we know, the fabric has a structure that can limit us or, on the other hand, advise us. We know that, up to a certain point, it is we who will decide how to move it, but from that point on it will be the fabric that chooses and finds the most natural path.

So, whenever we run into these problems, especially as regards the rigidity of the straight grain, we will make a cut. We will do it precisely at the point where we want the fabric to turn, rise, fall, open and close. Two cuts are always needed, allowing us to work the toile better and to distribute the opening of the cut evenly.

Each cut should always be made almost to the end of the fabric, leaving just 2 mm (0.078").

A very useful example for understanding this workaround, one of the first lessons for students of modelling, is to produce a flared skirt out of a basic pencil skirt. Just cut from the bottom of the skirt to the waist dart, close the dart and automatically the model will open and turn into a flared skirt. In the following exercises we will see the other possible solutions that can be obtained with a cut.

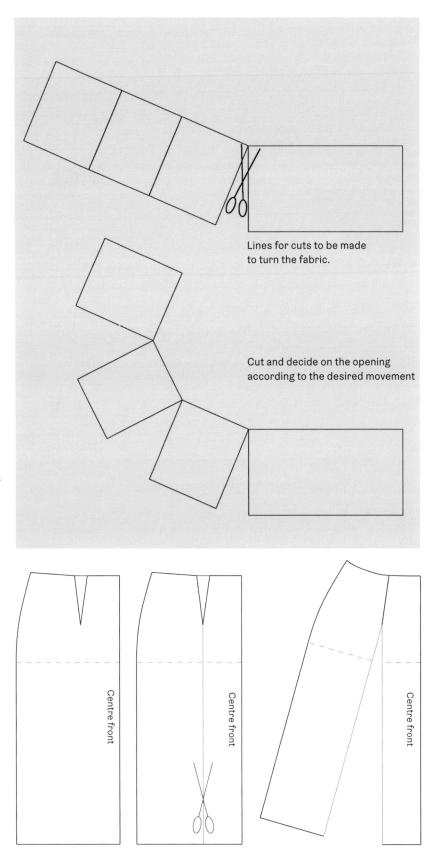

Lines for cuts to be made to turn the fabric.

Cut and decide on the opening according to the desired movement

Centre front

Centre front

Centre front

22

Industrialisation of the model

The model, after having been removed from the dress stand and balanced, is ready to be transferred to paper, arranged and simplified according to the rules of traditional modelling. This process is known as the Industrialisation of the model.

Proceed by marking the straight grain, which as we know will align with the direction of the warp, and all the various pieces, numbering them and specifying the front, the back, the right and left side, the various levels, and so on.

Where necessary level the seams, darts and levels, and add the seam allowances, which are always 1 cm (0.39"), except in the case of seams that turn where they are 7 mm (0.28") and are sewn to 5 mm (0.20"); this will allow us to make the fabric turn better, thus avoiding having to cut it.

Finally, mark all control points and simplify the model as much as possible, keeping the style and image of the garment intact.

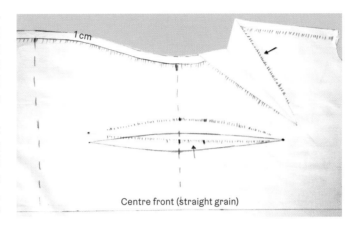

Centre front (straight grain)

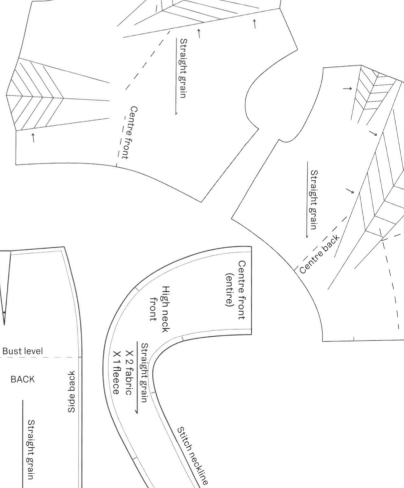

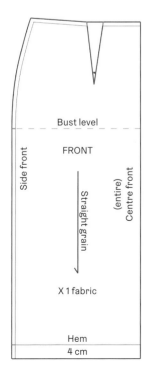

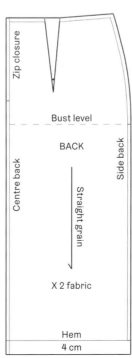

Research and study of the model

Before starting to model the toile or fabric on the dress stand, we need to choose the type of clothing (outerwear, dress, trousers, etc.), the line, the fit and the fabric with which to construct our creation. This will avoid wasting time and reduce the amount of toile used.

If we want to start creating from nothing or if we are short of ideas, as already mentioned in the introduction, we can use this technique to search for new lines and shapes, using the toile and modelling it until we obtain something that satisfies us.

Preparation of the toile to be modelled on the dress stand

To understand the technique and start working, we will create a classic symmetrical sheath dress, with a breast dart and a waist dart. So we will work on the straight grain, starting from the 1/2 front and then going to the 1/2 back. The toile used must have characteristics as similar as possible to those of the fabric we will use for the garment we intend to make. To make a knee length symmetrical sheath dress, cut out a rectangle of material with a width 1/4 of the greatest circumference of the size (being a size 42 EU / 14 UK, the largest measurement is the circumference of the hip) and a height equal to the length of the dress plus 10 cm (3.93").

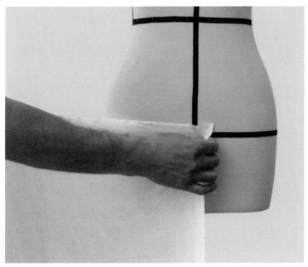

Position the toile at hip level 2 cm (0.78") from the centre front.

Measure 3 cm (1.18") beyond the side seam.

Make a cut and tear the toile.

2 cm

Bias

Straight grain

Always remember to iron the toile before you start modelling. Then, use a pencil to draw a parallel line 2 cm (0.78") from the edge, so as to obtain the centre front.

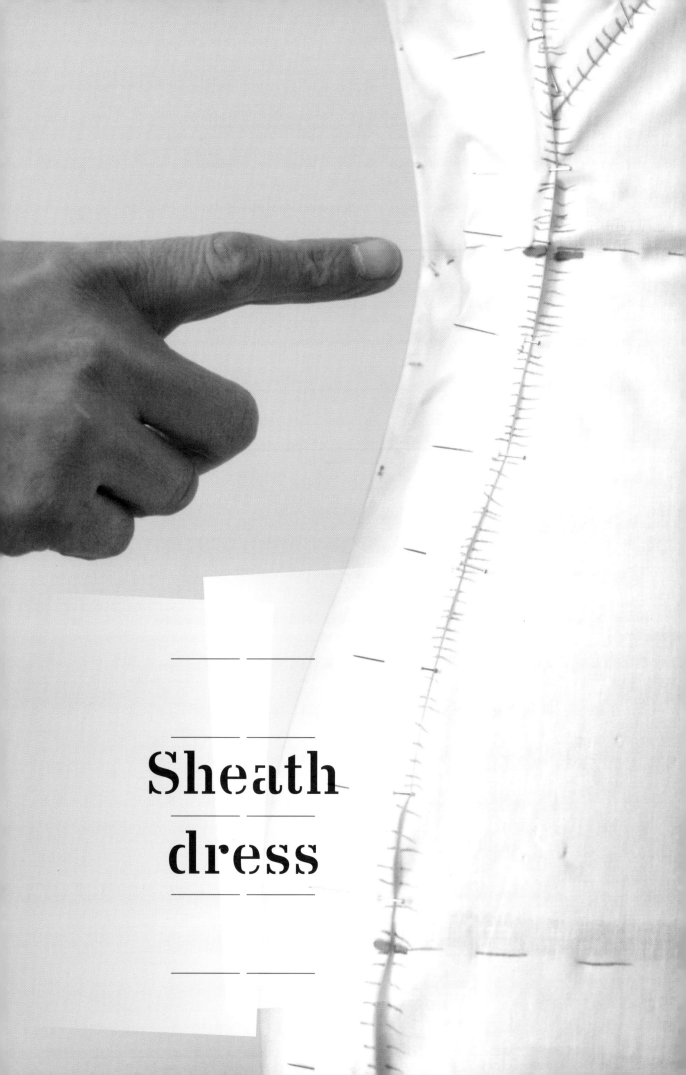

Sheath
dress

Positioning the toile
to be modelled

Now position the toile on the dress stand in alignment with the line we marked on the centre front of the dress stand. At this point secure the toile, first pinning the highest and lowest parts on the centre front which are then fully secured.

The pins should be positioned perpendicular to the vertical line, from right to left and, if you are left-handed, from left to right. They should sink into the toile, take hold of the webbing underneath and come out of the toile again. Remember the more pins you use the more precise the result.

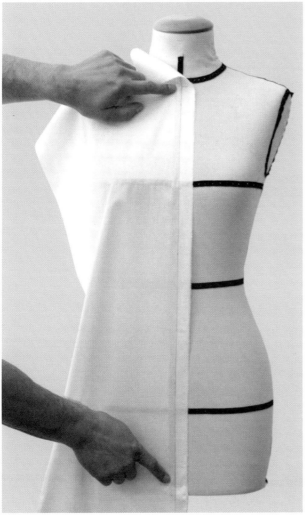

Pin the highest and lowest parts of the toile on the centre front.

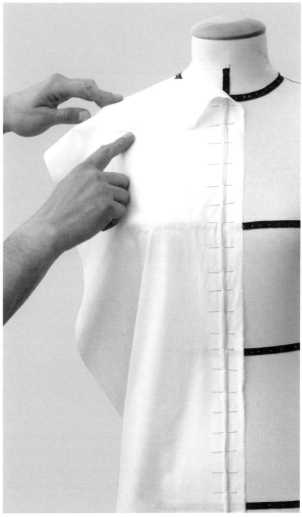

Now pin the entire toile on the centre front. The pins should be spaced at a maximum distance of 2-3 cm (0.78-1.18").

How to make darts

Having chosen to make a classic sheath dress with waist and bust darts, allow the toile to fall where there are no cuts or darts, in other words in the chest and hip area, and secure it with a pin (1). Now all the excess fabric is removed with darts.

First make the bust dart: take the excess toile at bust height, fold it and let it slip until you get the right amount of grip (2).

As you can see, the dart develops naturally up to the fullest point of the bust.

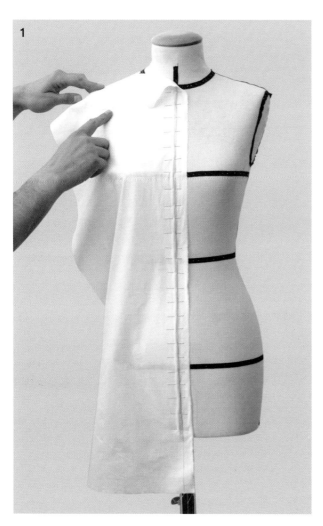

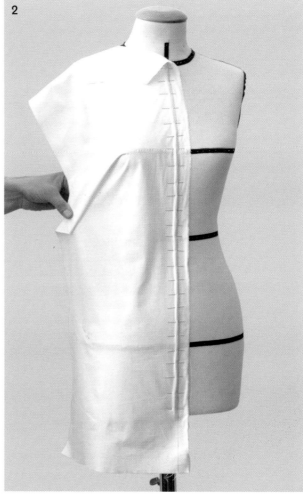

Tips

Handle the fabric gently, without forcing it too much, otherwise it could yield and fail.

You should move it as naturally as possible. Remember that fabric has its own structure: on the straight grain it becomes stiff and does not move, but if moved in other directions, such as the bias, it behaves in different ways (becoming soft, flowing and comfortable).

Let the fabric guide you and learn how to handle it, because you can decide how to move it up to a certain point, but from that point on it will be the fabric that chooses and finds a solution.

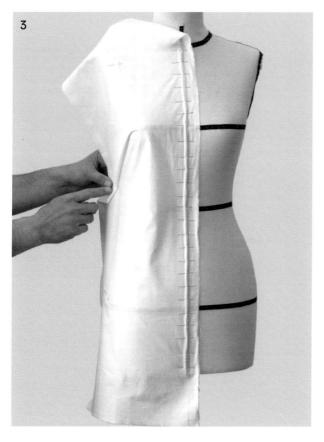

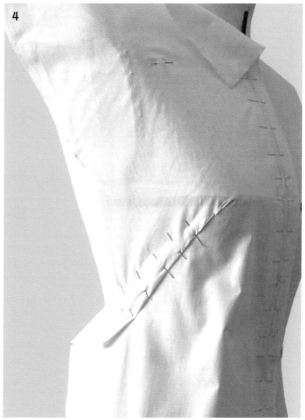

Once folded back, secure the fabric with a pin perpendicular to the dart, taking in only the folded layers of toile and not the dress stand (3).

From now on all seams, darts and cuts should be marked and secured with pins as shown in the figure, i.e. perpendicularly (4).

Now move on to the waistline dart: position yourself on the waist circumference line and pinch the toile until the desired fit is pared down and streamlined (5).

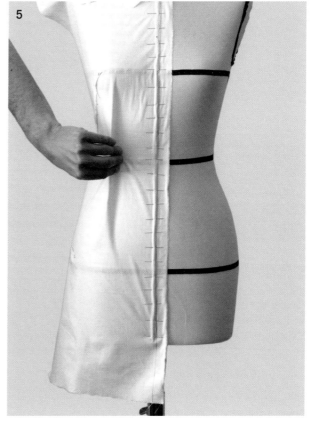

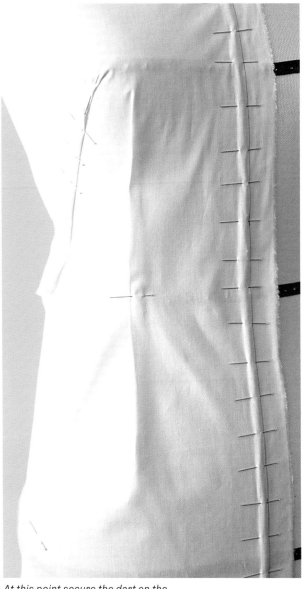

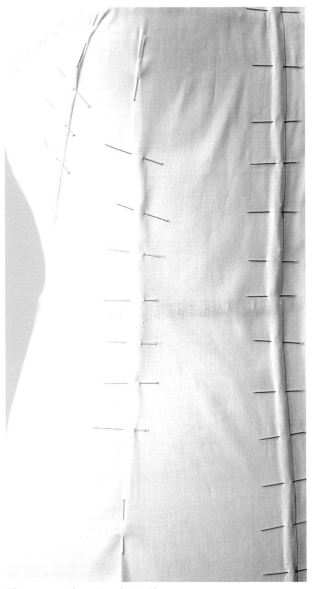

At this point secure the dart on the waistline with a first pin.

Then secure the entire dart with pins perpendicularly.

Once the first front half has been completed, make the back, where we will adopt the same method we used previously. Take the toile and position it at hip level 2 cm (0.78") beyond the centre back and 3 cm (1.18") from the side seam, and cut and tear it. Stretch the fabric and draw a parallel line 2 cm (0.78") from the edge of the toile to obtain the centre back which will be positioned on the webbing.

Once the 1/2 front and 1/2 back have been modelled, the fabric is trimmed and all the parts we don't need are removed (armhole, neckline, side front and side back). Remember to mark the clearance and cut taking into account the seam allowance (then working on a flat surface, when the model is balanced, the margins can be set exactly). Continue working by following the images on the facing page.

Make a vertical cut so the toile is correctly supported on the dress stand.

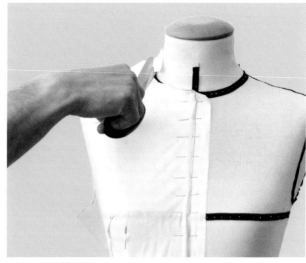

Cut the neckline leaving the seam allowances.

Mark the armhole.

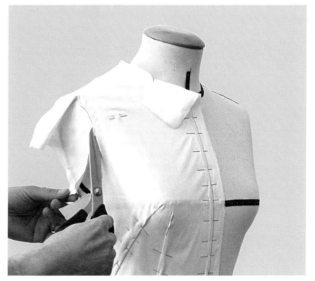

Cut the armhole leaving the seam allowances.

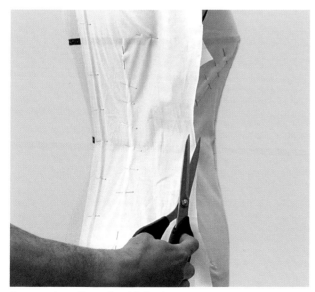

Remove the toile on the side back.

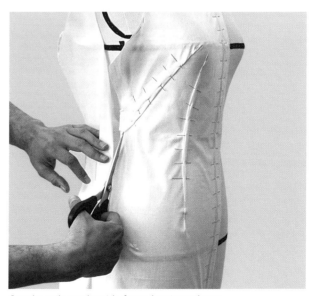

Cut the toile on the side front, leaving at least 2-3 cm (0.78-1.18") to better model the fabric.

How to join the front and back

Now we are ready to join the front and back. Whenever we have to assemble two or more pieces using a seam, the toile should be folded back and placed on the line where we want the seam to be.

In this case, since this is a simple sheath dress, use standard stitching, then the back toile is folded back and placed on the front toile precisely on the shoulder line and the side line.

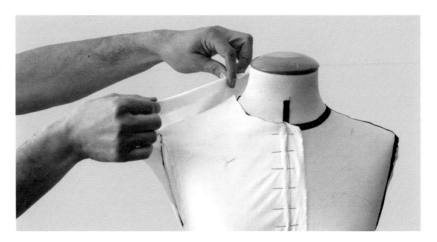

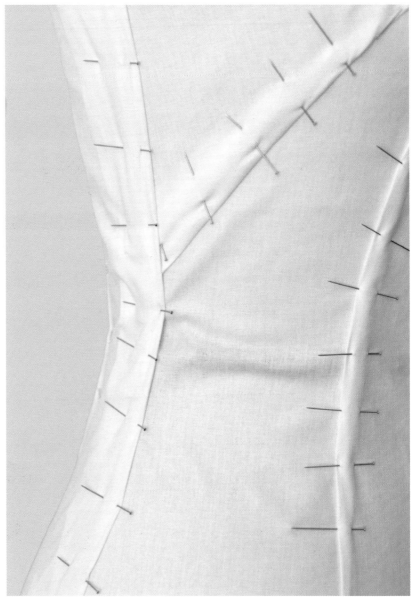

Fold back the fabric and place it on the line of the desired seam.

After folding back the toile, pin it entirely, always using the same method used for the darts (pins perpendicular to the seam).

Control points of the model

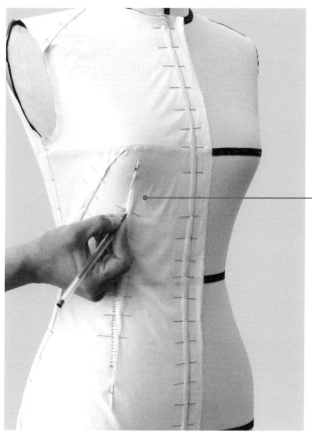
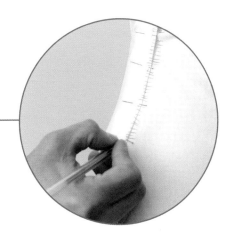

Make dotted lines at close intervals perpendicular to the dart, cut or seam.

After positioning the pins, mark small dotted lines at close intervals in pencil along the cutting lines and perpendicular to them, so as to mark both parts of the toile.

Mark all seams, cuts, darts, and all levels, bust, waist and hip. Mark all the principal stitching points with letters or numbers. This step will help us to reconstruct the model precisely.

The ends of the darts are marked with a dot.

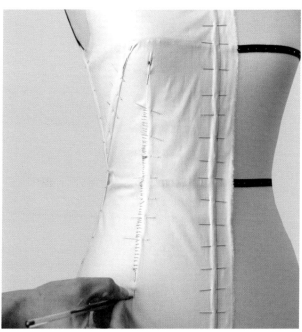

The ends of the darts should be marked with a dot 1 cm (0.39") from the end.

Sheath Dress

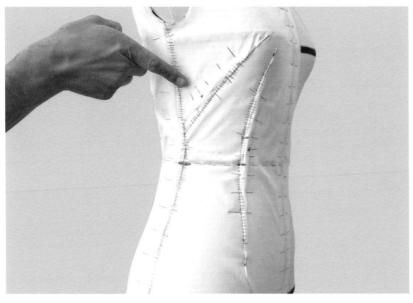

Before disassembling the model, perform an additional check. It is also important to mark the direction of the dart.

Mark all levels (bust, waist, hip) with a dotted line and draw a more marked red dotted line at the principal stitching points.

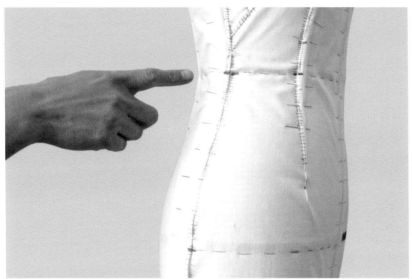

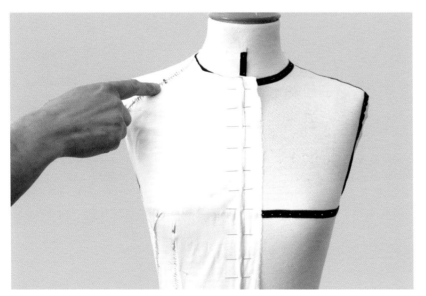

Since this is a simple sheath dress, there will be few control points to mark. If in future you are faced with a more complex model, I suggest using pencils and pens of various colours.

Industrialisation and drafting the pattern of the model

After marking all the points, start disassembling the toile. I suggest always taking a photograph of the prototype before disassembling it. Remove all the pins and smooth out the model with an iron. It is always advisable to make a series of checks to balance the garment. Finally, re-align the dart and add seam allowances where necessary.

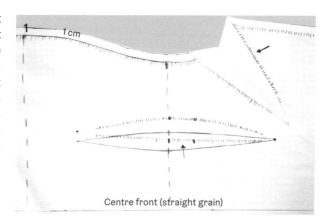

Centre front (straight grain)

(1) Restyle the dart at the waistline; as this is a standard sheath dress align it with the centre front.
This is not a rule, if you like the angle or the position of the one obtained previously, you may keep it.

(2) Balance the side seams and the hem, and then decide whether to flare the skirt or make it more snug.

(3) Restyle the clearance and add seam allowances.

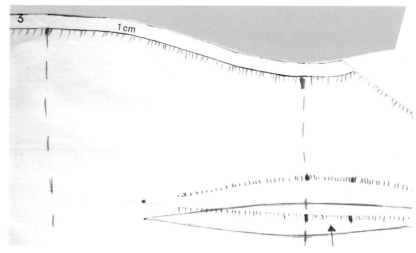

Assembly and testing of the toile-model

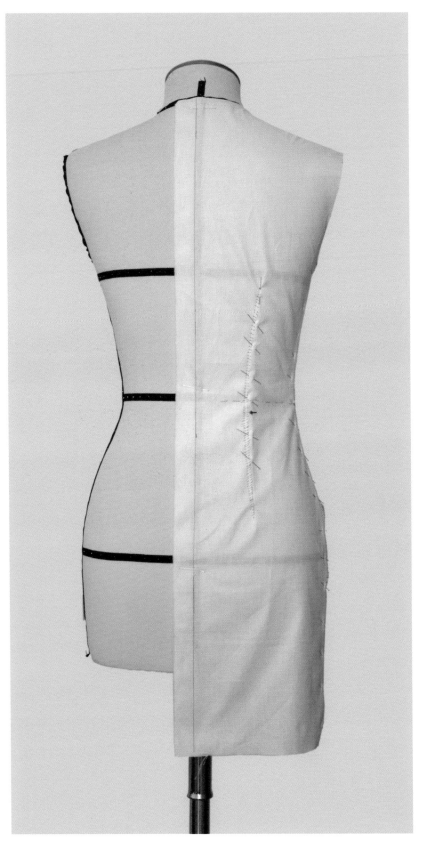

Having balanced and simplified the model, we are ready to reassemble and test our prototype. The garment should be reassembled using the same technique, always pinning using the same method, perpendicular to the cut-seam-dart, this time not on the dress stand but on the work table. Once assembled, try it out again on the dress stand to check the model.

Many of you will want to assemble the model with stitching, but my advice is to use pins, because if there are defects to be corrected, with the pins placed externally, we can remove the pin at any time, make the correction and replace it. If the style and fit reflect and fulfil our vision, the model is ready to be put onto paper.

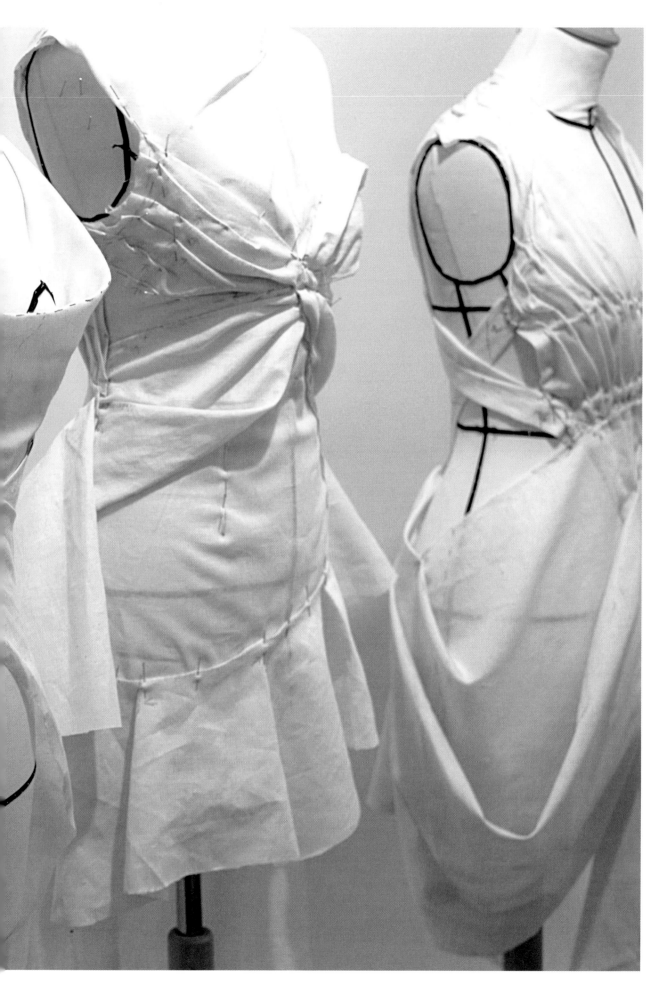

Cross pleats

Bodice with cross pleats

Before starting to model the toile, make a study of the model to understand how to proceed. We will do the same as we did on the sheath dress and mark all the control points, but this time we will do it on the picture or on the reference drawing we have to make.

As these are cross pleats, first mark the direction, count the number of pleats in order starting from the first to be mounted, and so on. Decide whether to work on the straight grain or in a more creative way (by positioning the fabric in a different way, like on the bias). For this model, with the upper part of the top smooth without pleats or darts, while the lower part is modelled with pleats and a cut on the left side, we have to work the toile on the straight grain; this is because having the straight grain on the centre front helps to give more stability to the garment.

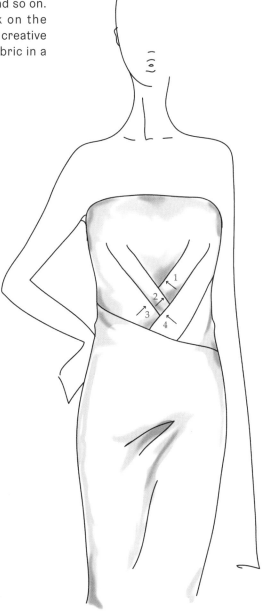

Preparation of the toile to be modelled

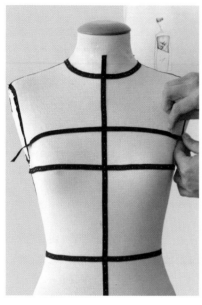

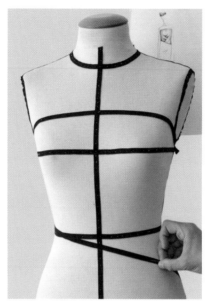

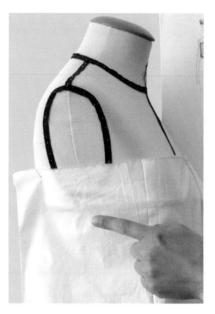

First define the area on which to work: position the webbing as a reference for the neckline and the bottom cut, and secure it with pins.

To make an approximate calculation of how much fabric we need, look at the drawing or photo and try to imagine loosening the pleats. The pleats on the model actually hide more fabric, so by undoing them you will see that there is more fabric on the sides.

At this point determine the widest circumference. Being a bodice,

the largest measurement is the bust circumference: divide this measurement into two adding 10-15 cm (3.93-5.90") more on the right and left side and mark the centre front with a line (which should align with the centre of the toile to be modelled). The height is given by the length measured from the highest point of the neckline of the bodice down to the lowest point of the bottom cut, always adding a few cm more 10-15 cm (3.93-5.90").

Position the webbing as a reference for the neckline and the bottom cut, and secure it with pins.

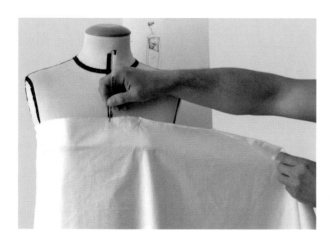

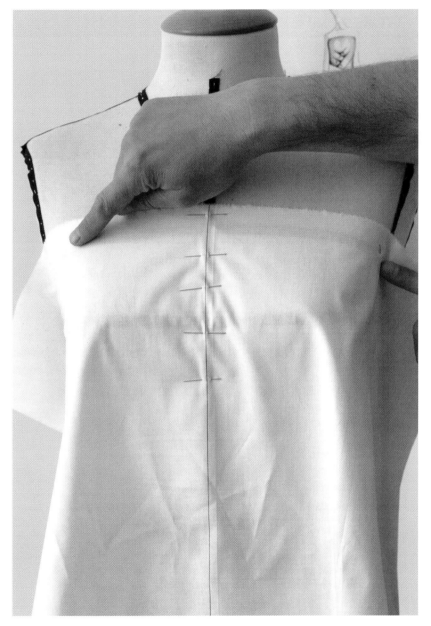

When the rectangle is ready, position it and secure it on the centre front of the dress stand. Remember that the pins are always attached perpendicularly. Now, given that the top part of the bodice is smooth with no cuts and no darts, allow the toile to fall in a natural way (as we did for the sheath dress, see pg. 27) and secure it with a pin on both sides. As you can see, the fabric naturally develops two large godet pleats.

In the following pages, the sequence of images will help us to understand how to interact and how to model the toile. Remember that there are no mathematical rules in Moulage: it is a technique that allows us to work directly on the dress stand, to secure the toile and mark the points.

Place the centre line of the toile on the centre front of the dress stand and secure it with pins. Allow the fabric to fall over the top part and secure with pins.

Tips

I suggest you learn how to move and model the toile because, as we already know, a stiff fabric, like our toile, has a structure with characteristics, which will condition us or make it easier to move it.

We know that on the straight grain the fabric becomes stiff and firm, like a piece of wood, while on the bias or out of the warp and weft, the fabric becomes more comfort-able, soft and flowing. For this reason it is sometimes preferable to work on the bias rather than on the straight grain.

How to cross the pleats

Going back to our model, which has a slim fit, take the large pleat on the right side and from its width we obtain 2 smaller pleats. Do the same thing with the godet pleat on the left side.

Next begin to give the pleats a direction, following the numbering shown on the drawing. First make pleat no. 1 which from the left must converge towards the centre, then pleats no. 2 and no. 3 which from the right go towards the centre, and, finally, pleat no. 4 which, in turn, will go from the left towards the centre.

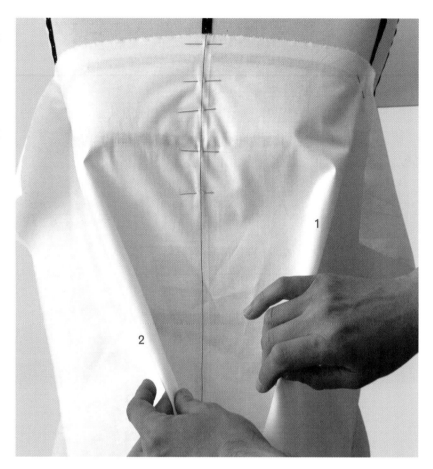

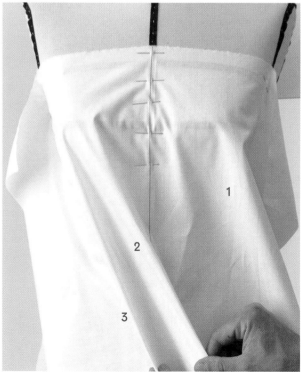

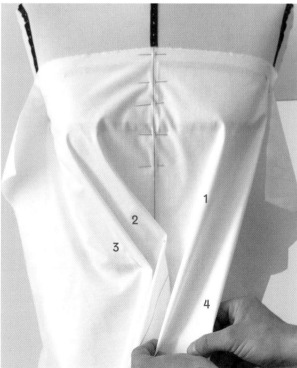

In this way we can see which direction we need to give to the fabric to start making the model.

As you can see, there is plenty of fabric that in some way we have to trim, but above all, these being cross pleats, we have to make a cut on the pleat bottom which will clear the way and make the fabric of the pleat that crosses over the other one more manageable.

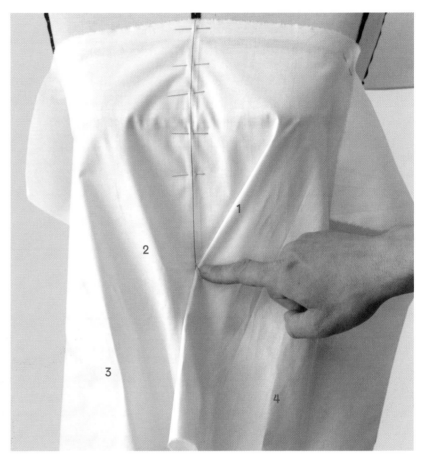

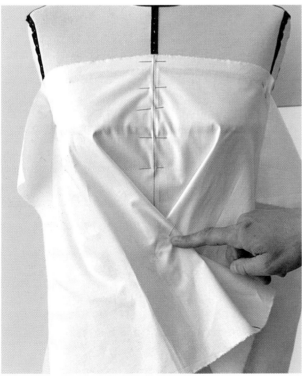

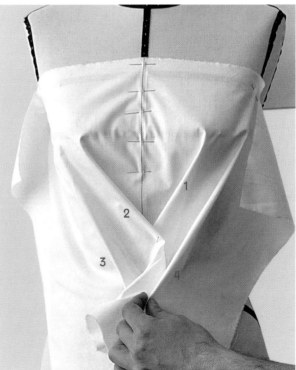

Locating the cut-pleat bottom

Start with the last pleat, no. 4. Always keeping the drawing in front of you with all the control points made in the model study phase, we can see that pleats no. 2 and no. 3 fit under the pleat bottom of no. 4. Then mark with a pencil the inside of pleat bottom no. 4: the line should go up to pleat no. 4.

Now get your scissors and cut pleat bottom no. 4 exactly on the line we just marked. Do the same thing with pleat no. 2: since pleat no. 1 fits under the pleat bottom of no. 2, mark the inside of pleat bottom no. 2.

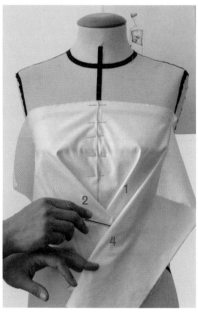

Mark with a pencil the inside of pleat bottom no. 4: the line should go up to pleat no. 2.

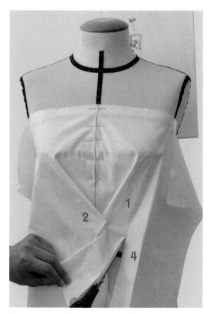

Cut pleat bottom no. 4 with scissors exactly on the line shown.

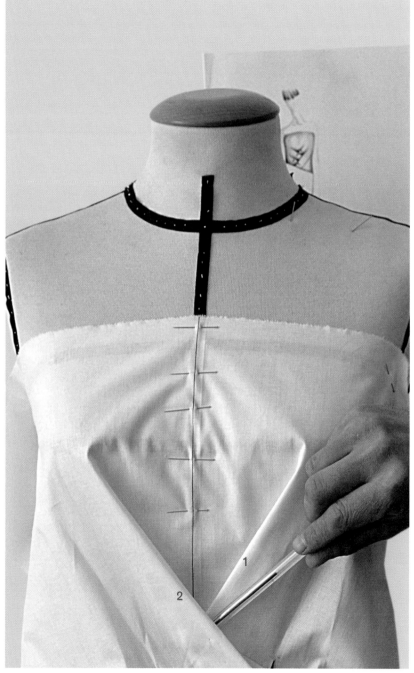

Mark with a pencil the inside of pleat bottom no. 2: the line should go up to pleat no. 1.

Get your scissors again and cut pleat bottom no. 2 exactly on the line we just marked.

Now we are ready to continue, close the pleats again following the numbering. Pleat no. 1 fits into the cut at the bottom of pleat of no. 2: then pleats no. 2 and no. 3 fit under the cut-pleat bottom of no. 4. Get some pins and firmly secure the pleats. Remember that the pins are always attached perpendicularly.

Cut pleat bottom no. 2 with scissors exactly on the line shown.

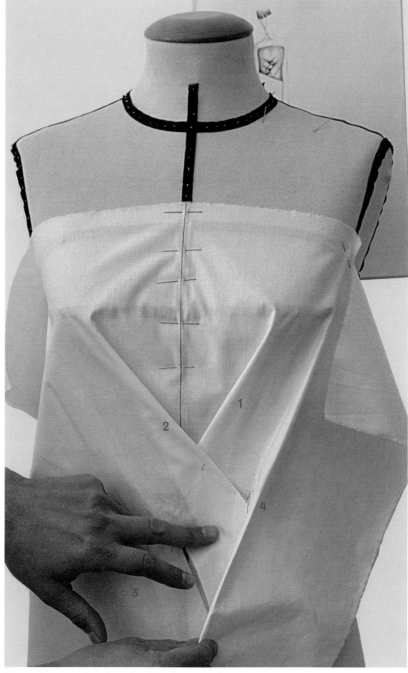

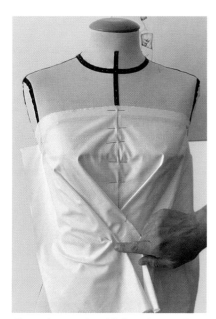

Close pleat no. 1 and fit into the cut of pleat bottom no. 2.

Close pleats no. 2 and no. 3 and fit them into the cut of pleat bottom no. 4.

Control points of the model

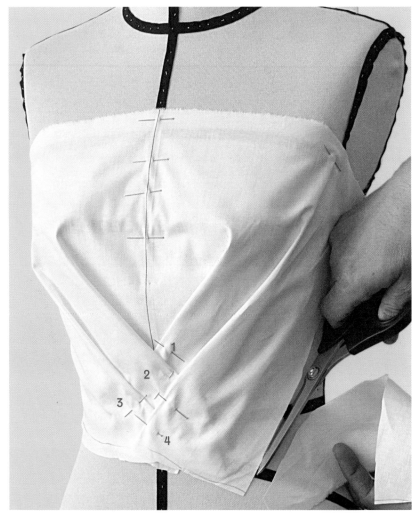

Before you start marking, remove any excess fabric you don't need: side, bodice bottom cut, etc. This helps the toile to adapt better.

As we have pleats that are close together, I suggest marking them with different colours.

Now we can start marking all the principal control points: the pleats, the direction of the pleats, their numbering and sequence, the neckline, the sides, etc

Remember to draw dotted lines at close intervals.

Remove the excess fabric (neckline, bottom cut, side seams, etc), leaving at least 2-3 cm (0.78-1.18") beyond the clearance, which we will use later to add the seam allowances.

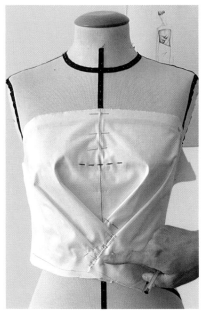
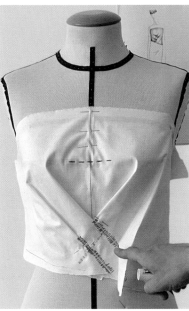
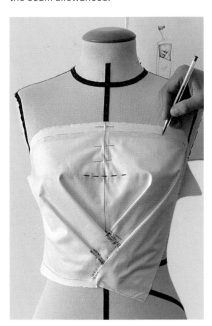

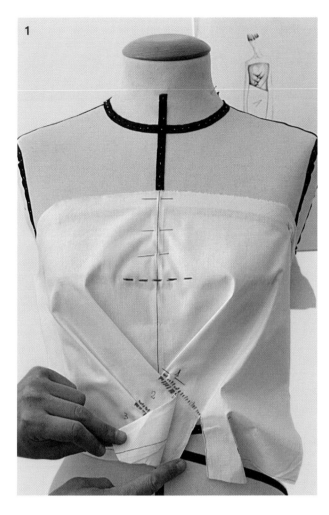

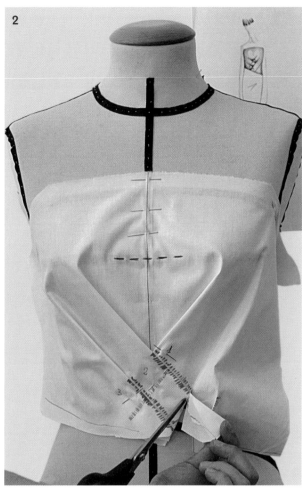

After marking all the control points, open the pleats again and remove the excess toile.

As shown in image (1), if pleats no. 2 and no. 3 cross over no. 4, cut them taking as your reference the cut of pleat bottom no. 4 (2).

Do the same thing with pleat no. 1 (3): cut them taking as your reference the cut of pleat bottom no. 2 (4).

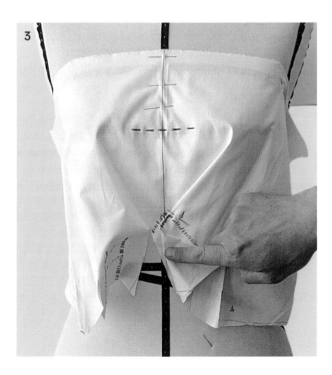

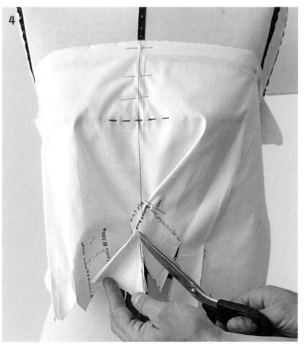

Completion of the model

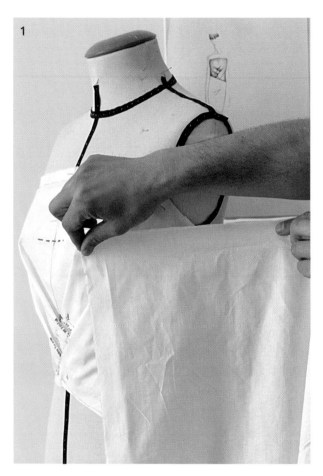

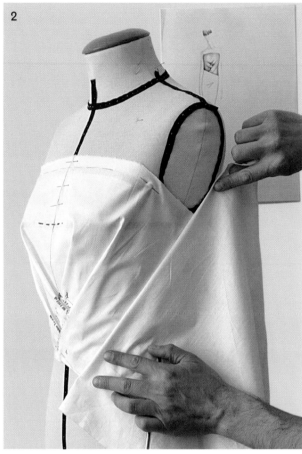

Close the pleats again. Having simplified and trimmed the toile, the model will acquire a fit and a style ever closer to our vision.

From the drawing we can see that there is a cut on the left side. Every time we add a new piece, module or cut, we must decide how to position the toile, whether to put it on the dress stand on the straight grain (1), or place it respecting the direction of the already mounted toile (2).

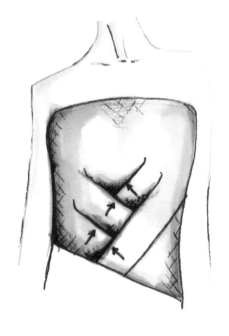

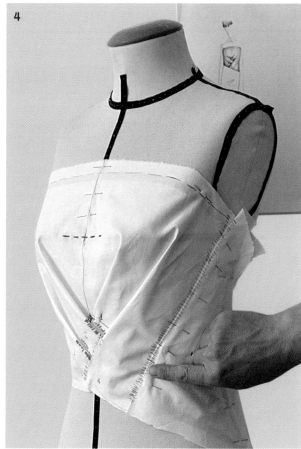

In this case, we decide to work it respecting the direction of the already mounted toile. Once arranged on the dress stand, we have to make the seam. Remember what we did in the first Sheath Dress model (see pg. 32): at the point where the seam will be, fold back 2 cm (0.78") of the toile, resting it on the cut as shown in the drawing.

Secure with pins placed perpendicular to the cut and remove the excess toile (3).

Mark the entire seam of the cut with dotted lines, make a notch with a clearer mark in red at the centre of the cut-seam and show all the other necessary control points (4).

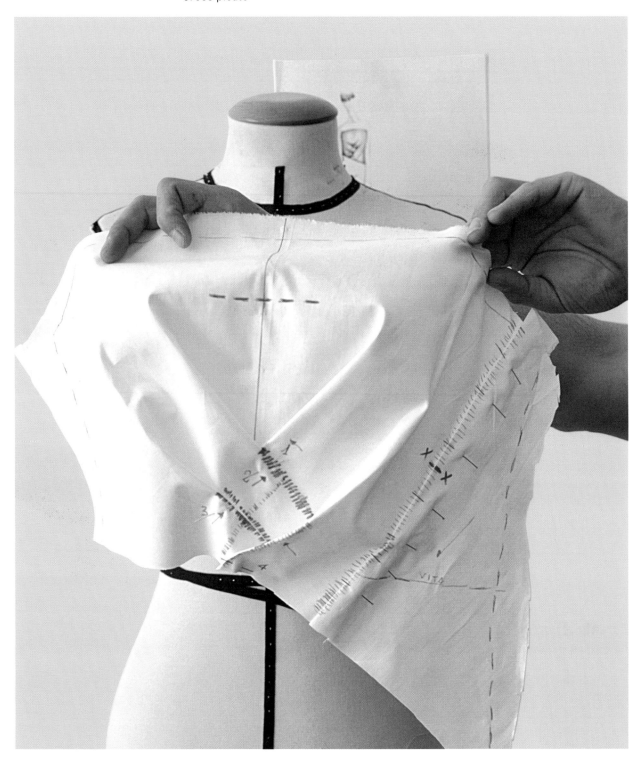

The model can now be detached from the dress stand (it is important to detach it fully assembled so you can check the inside). Then you can think of how to tailor and create the bodice.

Of paramount importance, but we won't do as an exercise, is the lining that we can make at all times.

Tailoring solutions

To complete the model we should already be thinking of how to tailor it. This step is very important, since the choice we make could influence and change the shape of the model. To construct it we used the technique of Moulage, but now, thinking about the finished garment, we have to re-place the pins with a seam. The problem would be solved immediately by making a seam on the application, but since we want to make a clean bodice without visible stitching, but with hidden seams, we will proceed as shown in the following photos.

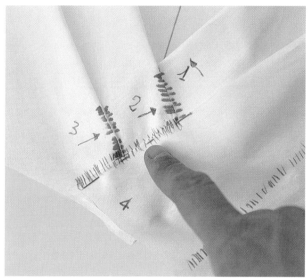

Put the pins flush into pleat no. 4.

Turn the model upside down from the inside and mark at 1 cm (0.39) from pleat reference no. 4, continuing in an L shape to close the pleat.

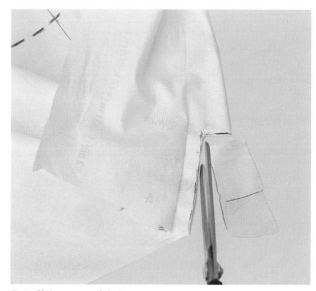

Cut off the excess fabric.

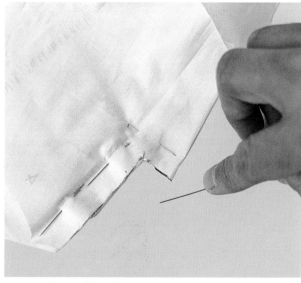

Remove the pins from the outside and reposition them on the inside where the seam will go.

Industrialisation and drafting the pattern of the model

This is the completed model. It could already be used, but it would be better to arrange all the lines with the due seam allowances, balance it and mark the various control points before putting it onto paper.

The model is ready to be reassembled and re-tested on the dress stand to see if there are any further defects to correct.

Once you have reassembled it and checked it is all correct, you can put it onto paper.

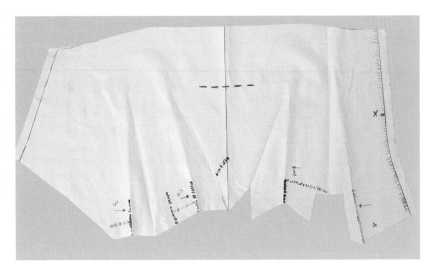

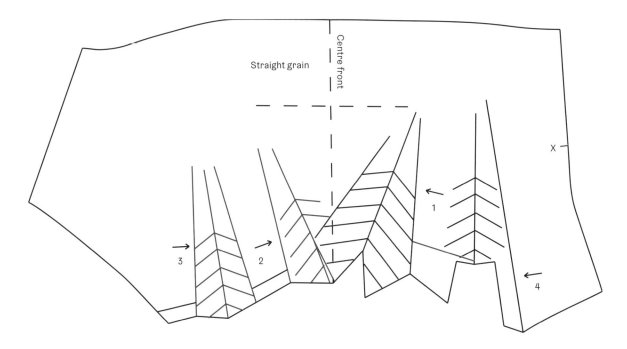

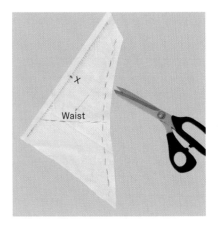

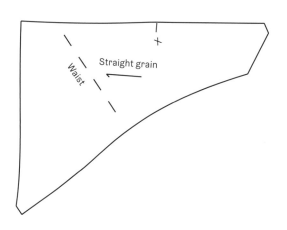

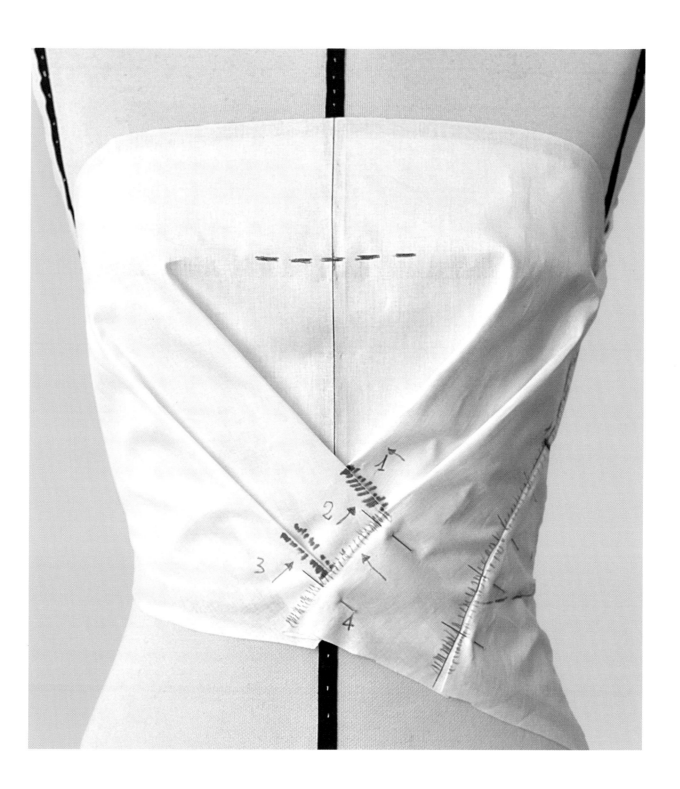

One shoulder
bodice

Asymmetrical one shoulder bodice

Remember, before you start modelling the toile, make a study of the model. Decide whether to work on the straight grain or in another way and mark the direction of the pleats and drapes.

Looking at the drawing of the front we can see two pleats: one that creates a one-shoulder and one at the waist. The back has a large pleat that becomes the one shoulder and a pleat on the shoulder.

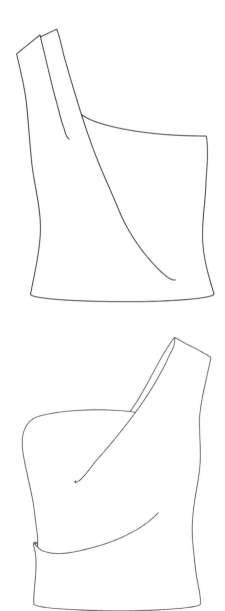

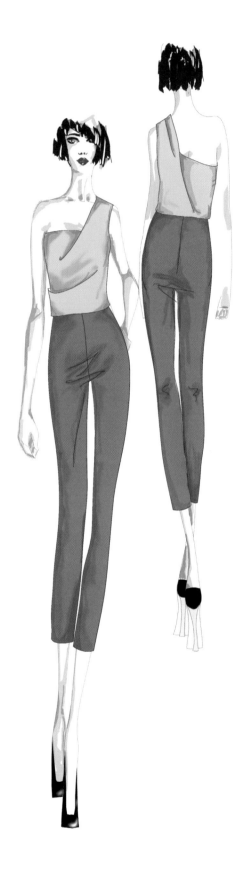

Learning how to move the toile

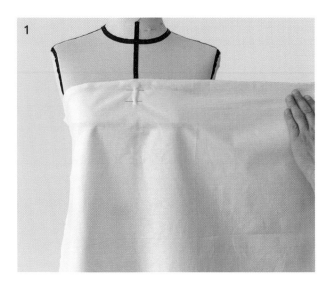

After studying the model and cutting the rectangle, position the centre of the toile on the straight grain on the line of the centre front and secure top part of the toile with 4-5 pins (1). Looking at the drawing, first do the left shoulder: take the end of the toile and gently pull it upwards (2), then rest it on the left shoulder in the desired position. Now secure it with pins (3).

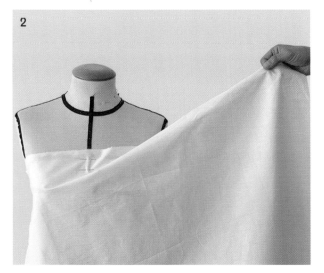

Now for the lower right side pleat. Hold the toile at one point (4) and move it upwards: a pleat will emerge which, in addition to reflecting the idea of style, must have the function of streamlining the toile at the waist until you get the desired fit. Once the pleat is done, secure the first part with 3-4 pins perpendicularly (5), otherwise continue modelling the toile, moving the fabric in a different way until you achieve the desired model.

Now, after having secured the pleat on the right side, on the left shoulder and on the sides, remove the excess toile.

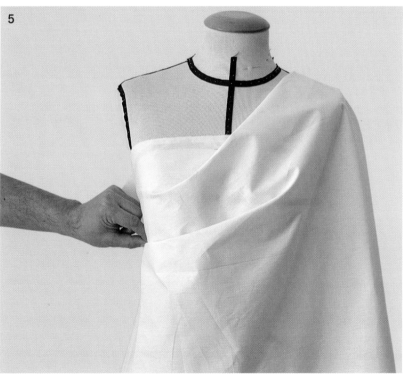

Tips

Remember that the toile-fabric has a structure and may be compared to a set of ropes: you have to find the right rope and move it until you achieve the intended style and fit.

Moulage allows us to intervene in any way and at any time.

Working on the dress stand you can remove and attach the pins as and where you want, it will be your idea or drawing of what you want to create that will guide you.

Again, remember that you need to learn how to move the fabric and

let it guide you, because you can decide how to move it and turn it how you want up to a certain point, but from that point on it will be the fabric that decides.

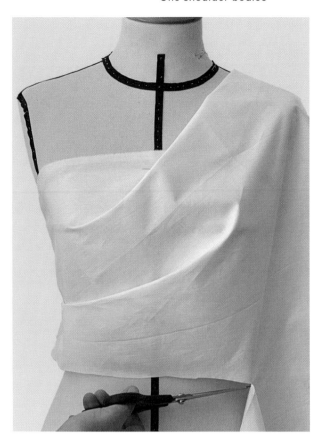

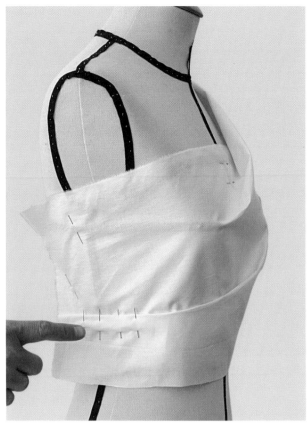

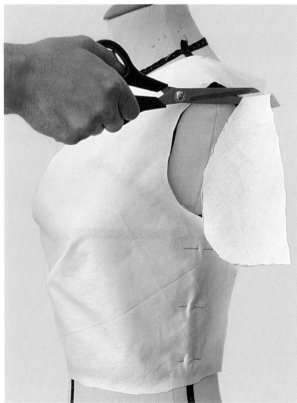

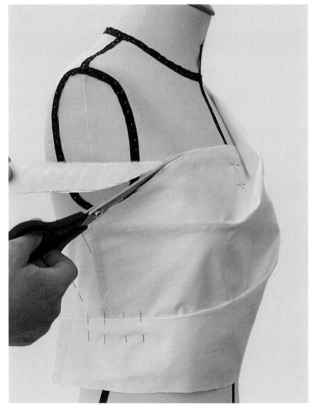

Before cutting the excess toile, mark with a pencil the part to be removed, remembering not to cut on the clearance, but always leaving the seam allowances.

Try to work in a precise way from the beginning, even if afterwards, once the model has been disassembled and balanced, you will rearrange everything with a ruler, set square and French curve.

One shoulder top back

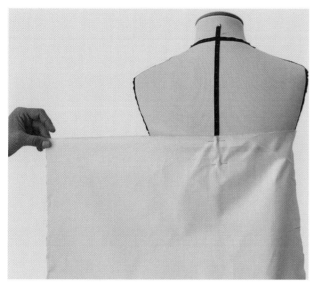

Hold the end of the toile.

Move the toile upwards.

As for the front, after studying the model, cut the toile and secure it on the centre back.

Then gently pull up the end of the toile and rest it on the desired point.

Remember that the toile-fabric has a structure and may be thought of as a set of ropes: you have to find the right rope and move it until you achieve the desired result.

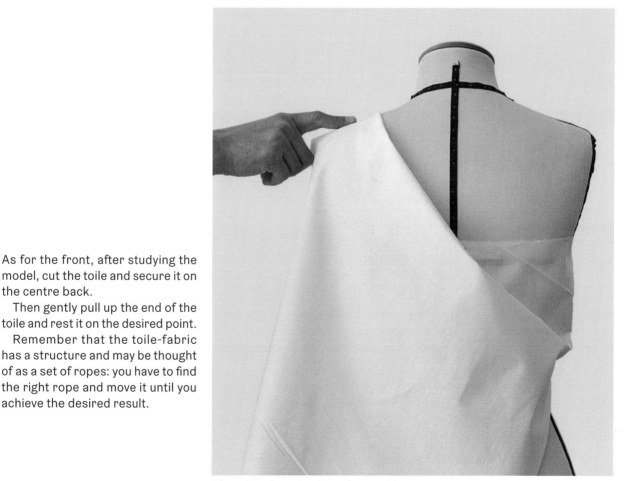

Place the toile on the desired point of the shoulder and secure with pins.

One shoulder bodice

To make the pleat on the shoulder, hold the toile at one point and move it to the right.

Once the pleat is made, secure it with pins perpendicularly.

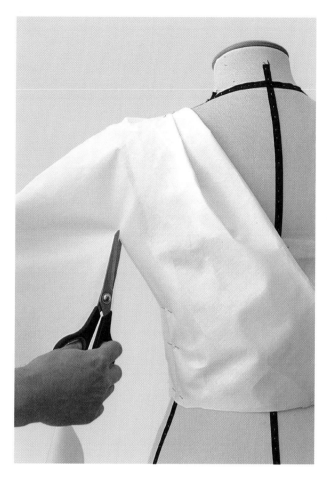 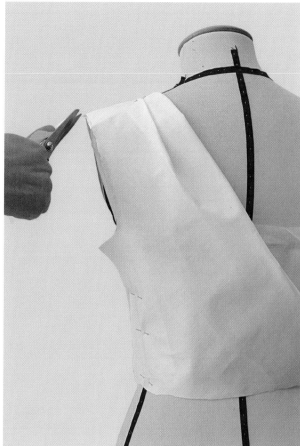

Remember while working to always trim the excess toile, this will help you to work in a precise way and to create your model perfectly.

After you have finished modelling the front and back, you have to combine them: the method is the same as that used in the previous creations.

Take hold of the toile of the bodice back, fold it and rest it on the bodice front where you want the seam. This applies to both the shoulder seam and the seams of the right and left side (where the zip will be fitted).

Remember to always pin it all using the same method (pins perpendicular to the seam).

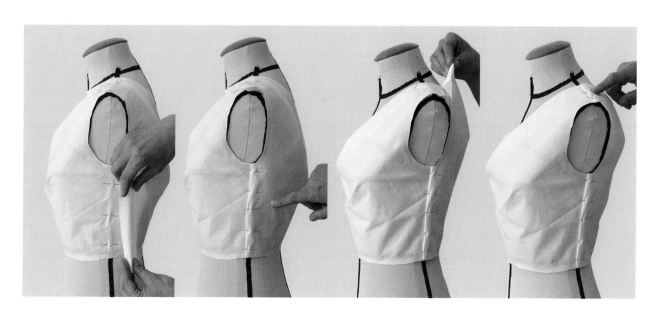

Control points of the model

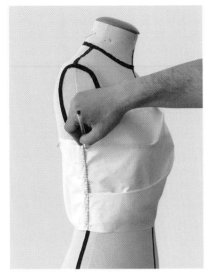
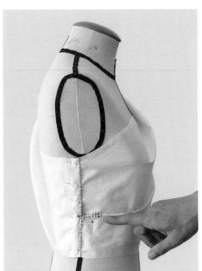

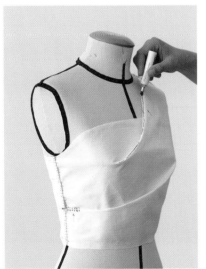
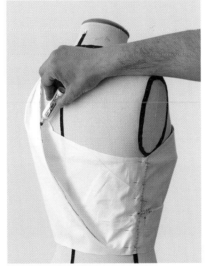

Now we are ready to start marking all the control points needed to make the model.

Mark all the seams with dotted lines, as in the previous creations, and the start of the pleat with red dotted lines.

Now mark a new control point on the large pleat that becomes the shoulder. As shown in the following images, mark the protruding part of the pleat with a red marker and the pleat bottom with a pencil. This applies to both the front shoulder pleat and the back shoulder pleat.

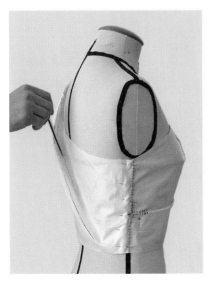
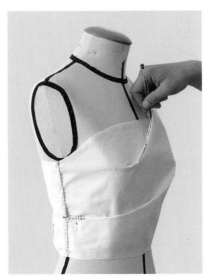

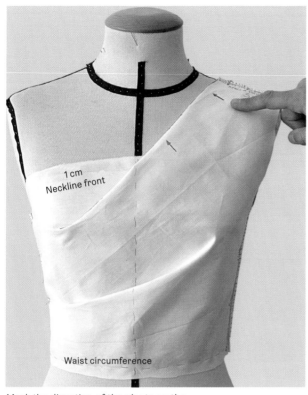
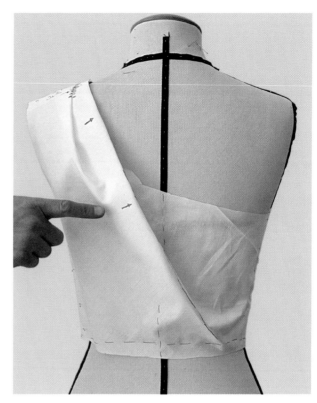

Mark the direction of the pleats on the front and back with arrows.

Use a pencil to draw a dotted line on the centre front, on the centre back, at bust level and at waist level.

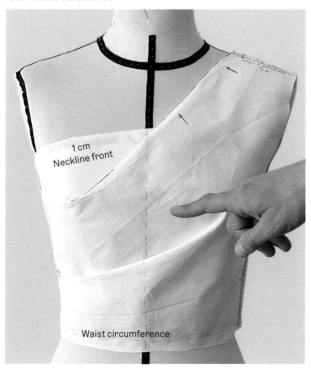
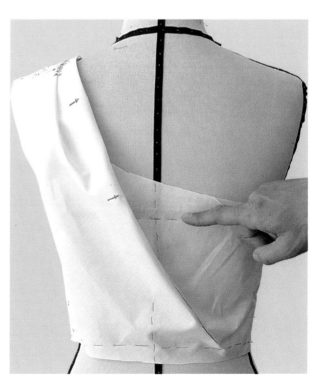

Industrialisation and drafting the pattern of the model

Once you have finished marking, remove the pins on the zip side and remove the model from the dress stand. Check everything, disassemble it and balance it.

After placing the model on the table, add the seam allowances and all the lines with a ruler, set square and French curve, and mark all the control points in the usual way, including the pleats.

The model is ready to be put onto paper or digitised with Cad software.

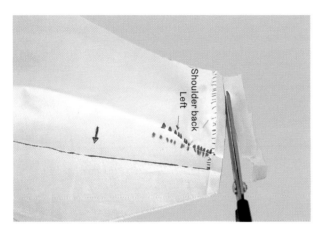

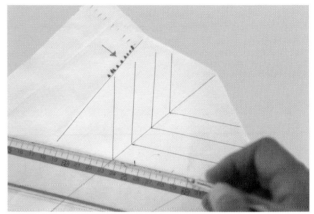

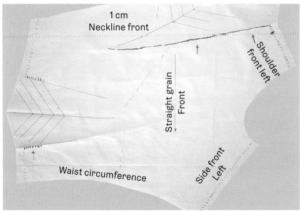

Front

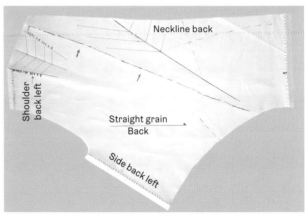

Back

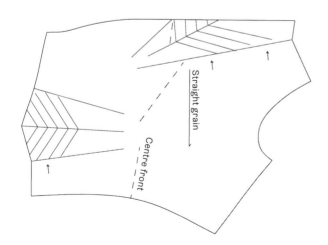

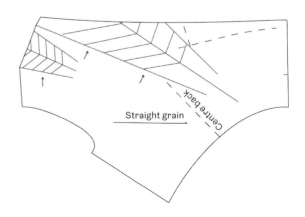

One shoulder bodice

Draping

How many times have we tried to reproduce a drape or simple pleats with modelling? Almost always, after transferring the pattern onto the fabric and mounting the garment, we do not obtain the desired effect, the pleats or the drape do not remain in the expected position. Working directly with the fabric allows us to manage style and fit at all times.

The point is always the same: you have to learn how to move the fabric in the right direction. Once again it is useful to imagine the toile as a set of criss-crossed ropes: to have a pleat or a volume in a certain position you need to pull the right rope. The movement must be natural without forcing the fabric too much: it must stay where we want without pulling or stressing the toile. As already said many times, the fabric has its own structure, we can decide how to move it up to a certain point. Try to handle a firm (non-stretch) fabric: it has straight grain in the weft and in the warp, so if we pull the fabric in line with these we will see that the toile does not move, it remains firm. If the movement is unsatisfactory, undo the pleat and move the fabric from a different position.

Draped one shoulder dress

Before you start modelling the toile, make a study of the model. Decide whether to work on the straight grain or in another way, locate the seams, mark the direction of pleats-drapes, etc.

Looking at the design we can see that the dress is a one shoulder draped on the right side, while on the left side of the bust area we have pleats that transmit precision and rigidity, so they will be worked on the straight grain. As we will see shortly, we will use an iron and a thermoadhesive toile to help us. In some cases, these pleats may also be modelled directly on the dress stand, working the toile on the bias.

How to create the drape

Hold the toile at the corner and let it fall naturally: thanks to the force of gravity the toile will collect at the bottom and form a series of pleats, similar to the rays of the sun (1). This will help you understand, each time you make a drape, how to position the toile and how to start modelling it.

Looking at the drawing, you can see that the ray starts from the shoulder, so hold the corner of the toile and secure it behind the right shoulder (2). Depending on how many pleats or gathers you want to have on the shoulder, you need to raise or lower the position of the toile (3).

Now hold the toile at hip height on the left side, gently move it upwards (4), approximately up to waist level, and we secure it with pins (5).

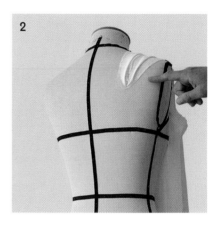

As already seen in the previous creations, you can continue to model the fabric until you achieve the desired movement, removing and attaching pins at all times.

Tips

If you have two or more drapes, so more points from where the rays will start, you will preferably have to start working from the highest one, for the reasons explained above related to the force of gravity and the weight of the toile. Remember that a proper handling of the toile can make all the difference.

Hold the toile on the right side just below the waist and pull it upwards until it forms pleats-drapes. Remember that once your idea of the style is satisfied, you have to think about the fit, so when modelling the pleats, try to achieve the perfect shape. Remember to always secure your completed work with 3-4 pins attached perpendicularly at the start of the pleats.

Our model is starting to take shape. Now go to the left side: hold the toile and pull it upwards until it forms pleats-drapes, try to fulfil the image of the drawing and secure the start of the pleats with 3-4 pins attached perpendicularly.

Hold the toile just below the waist and pull it gently upwards.

Secure with pins.

Hold the toile in line with the hip and pull it gently upwards.

Secure with pins.

Hold the toile just below the waist and pull it gently upwards.

Secure with pins.

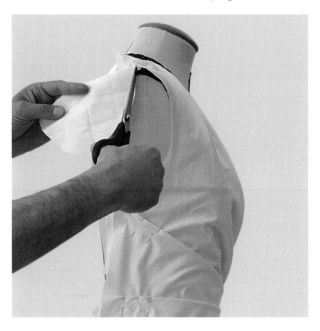

Before continuing, it is important to remove all the excess toile, i.e. the side, armhole, shoulder, and wherever necessary.

When we have a model with pleats or drapes that cross over, remember to make a cut inside the pleat-drape bottom, so as to remove the excess toile to help you to work it in a more natural and clean way and avoid an accumulation fabric.

Open the pleats above the left side.

Make a cut in the pleat bottom (see Cross pleats exercise, page 44).

After removing the excess toile, reposition the drape. Hold the toile at the point shown previously and pull it gently upwards.

Continue adjusting the model, trying to simplify it as much as possible, but keeping the concept of style clear. A lot of fabric is left over from the cut made previously in the pleat bottom that you should let fall naturally downward. You can see that in the skirt section on the left side there is a lot of width which you will reduce in order to reproduce perfectly the model shown in the drawing.

Lift the toile again and make a cut to remove any excess. It is always advisable to make the cut along the line of the straight grain so that when tailoring everything is made easier and more precise. We already know that seams stitched on a straight grain fabric are stronger than those stitched on the bias and around it, where the structure of the toile yields naturally.

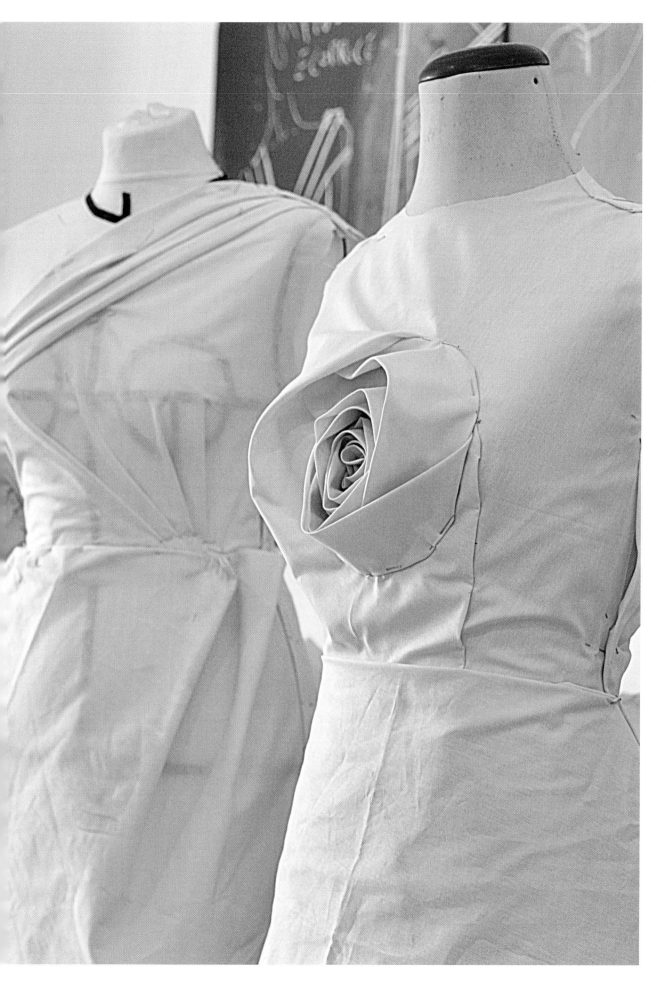

Pleats on the straight grain

Once the drape is finished, start working the pleats on the left side of the bust. In the model study phase we decided to work them on the straight grain even if, as mentioned above, you could work them on the bias. To cut the rectangle to be modelled, place the toile at bust height and measure the widest point between the one shoulder seam-cut and the side, remembering to add 3-4 cm (1.18-1.57") on either side.

The height of the rectangle to be modelled is obtained from the area to be covered plus the number of pleats.

Lay your work flat on the table and mark the control points of the pleats with a line.

Take the toile and position it on the ironing surface. With the help of the control points taken previously, make the first pleat, secure the end

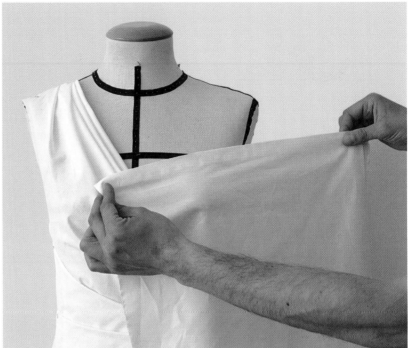

with a pin and flatten the entire fold with an iron. Repeat the operation several times until you have the desired number of pleats.

Before modelling the pleats on the dress stand, you need to secure them together so they won't open. To do this you could use adhesive tape, but since we want to simulate the yield of the pleats with their final fabric, we will use an adhesive fleece.

Then turn the fabric, take some thermoadhesive fleece and apply it to the pleats with an iron.

The pleats can now be modelled directly on the dress stand.

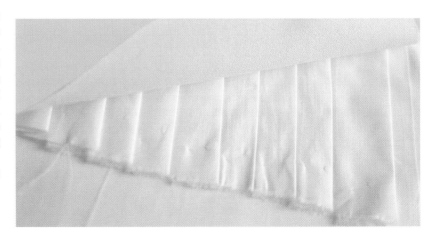

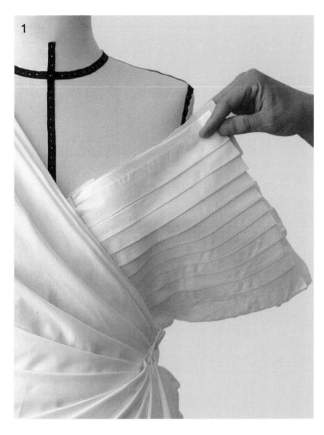

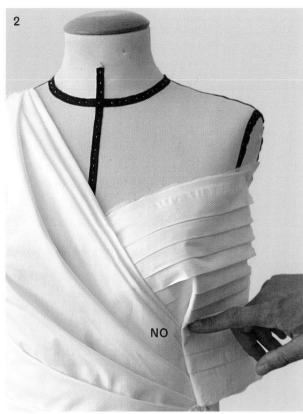

Position the pleats on the dress stand at left bust height and fit them under the toile where the seam-cut will be and on the left side.

You can see that the pleats, being on the straight grain, remain rigid and do not adhere to the dress stand (1). The model, however, is semi-adherent, so we need to add a dart. Fig. 2 shows what should not be done in this case!

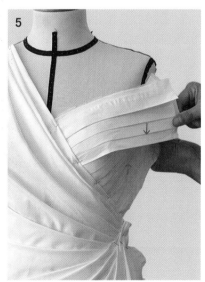

This exercise helps us to understand how Moulage and modelling are not mutually exclusive techniques, but rather they aid and complement each other. For example, when during modelling we have to move a bust dart to the shoulder, we have to close the old dart with adhesive tape and cut at the exact point where we want the dart to be transferred. As we know, in modelling it is possible to tilt the bust dart into any position within a perfect circle (360°).

In the exercise shown in the images, in order not to undo the pleats and make the dart invisible, you must mark under the pleat bottom up to the most prominent point of the bust (3). Cut along the measured line (4) and slide the pleats under the cut upwards and those above it downwards (5).

After securing the pleats together and assembling the pieces with pins attached perpendicular to the cut-seam, prepare the neckline and the side.

At this point, having prepared the model and attached the pins, the toile is ready to be marked.

Control points of the model

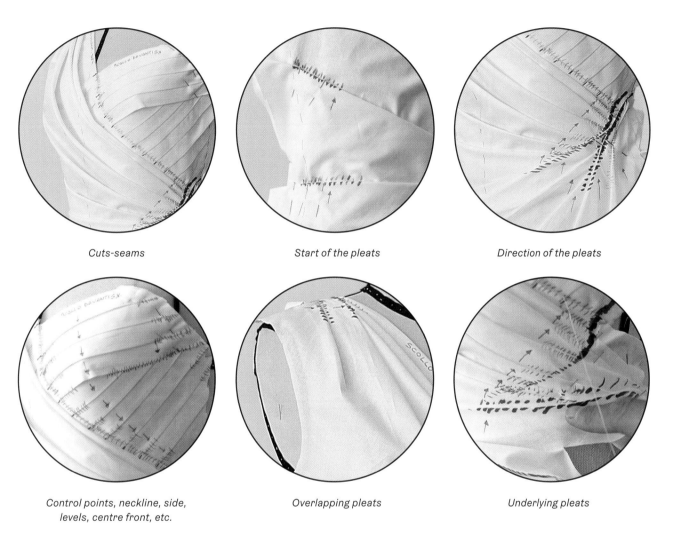

Cuts-seams

Start of the pleats

Direction of the pleats

Control points, neckline, side, levels, centre front, etc.

Overlapping pleats

Underlying pleats

Use coloured pens to mark everything: remember that the pleats, the darts and the cuts-seams must be marked with continuous dotted lines.

Remember that after having marked all the control points, before disassembling the pleats-drapes and drafting the pattern of the model, you need to cut the excess toile respecting the seam allowances, so as to obtain the right shape in the pleat-drape bottom.

Industrialisation and drafting the pattern of the model

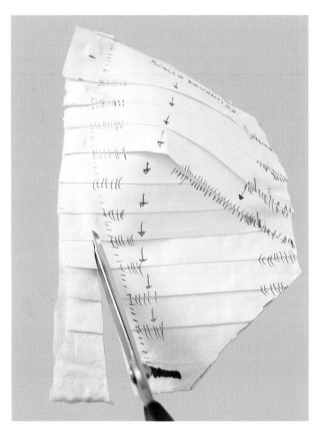

After marking everything you can remove the pins and disassemble it. I suggest removing one piece at a time: disassemble a couple of pleats and reassemble them, if everything is right, disassemble other ones and reassemble them. This will help us to see if there are other things to mark underneath or sections of the toile to be removed, but also to gain confidence in performing everything correctly.

Remove the excess toile for the dart considering the seam allowances.

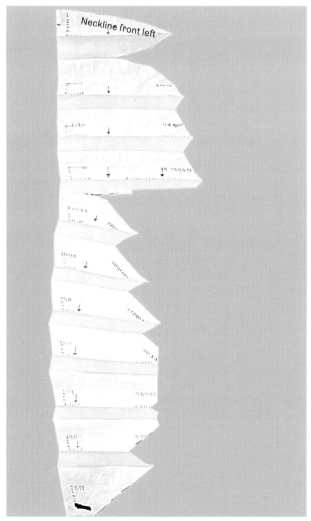

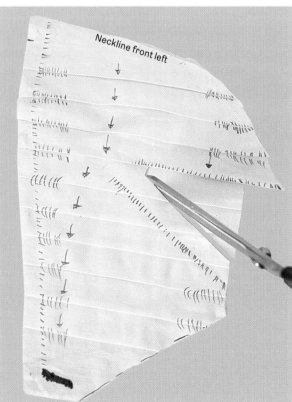

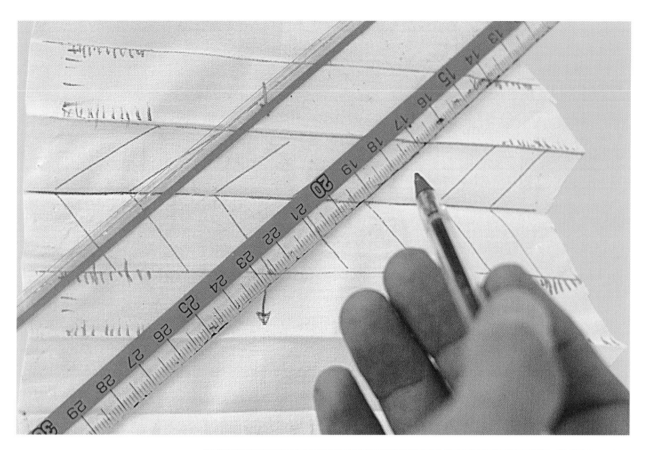

Arrange and mark the pleats as in the modelling.

Before opening the drape, check that everything has been marked. Also add the numbering of the pleats-drape assembly sequence.

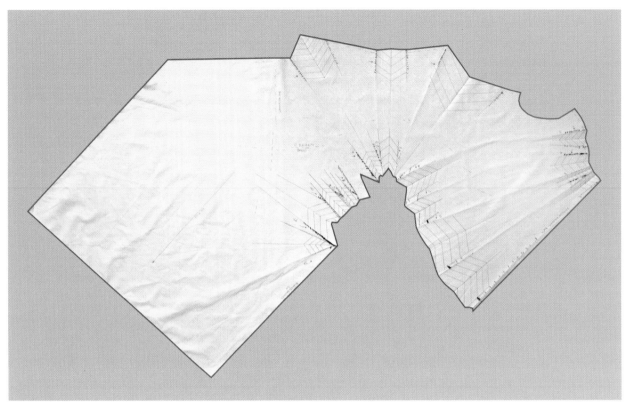

Draping

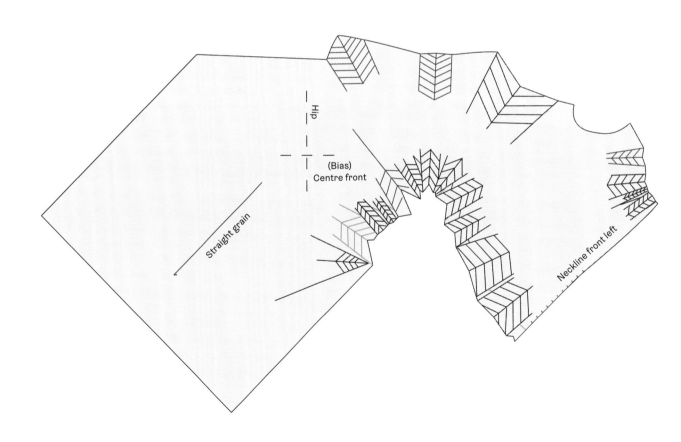

Knots

Top with knot under the bust

When it comes to knots, the first thing that comes to mind are two fabrics that turn, cross over and fit together. There are different ways of turning and knotting fabrics together: they can be positioned anywhere, although for reasons of functionality they are usually placed under the bust, on the shoulder or on the thigh at hip level. When two portions of fabric intersect with each other, another two strips of fabric are formed (four in total) that we will learn how to manage.

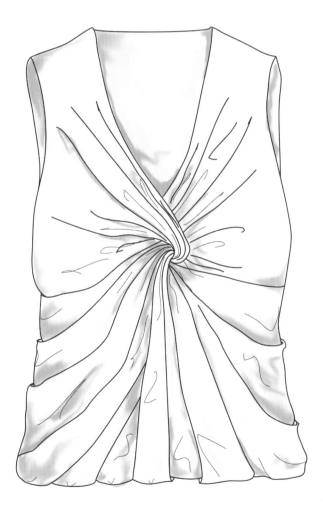

Preparation of the toile to be modelled

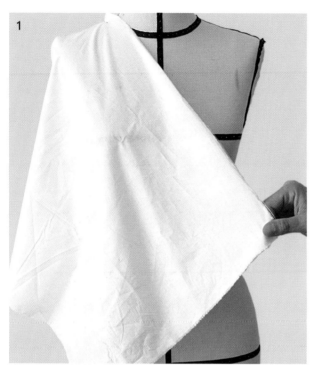

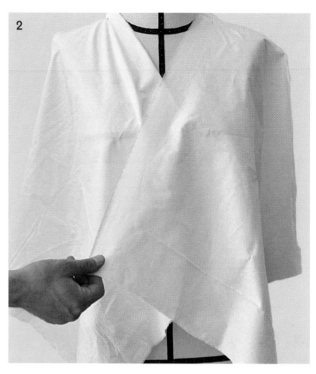

To make a top with a knot under the bust we will work on both sides of the dress stand (right and left), but if we want to get a symmetrical garment we will then have to choose the side we like best and duplicate it, so as to work in a mirror-like manner. In this case, to practise modelling the toile, we will work to the end with the two sides.

Put the toile on the dress stand and pull it gently from the corner opposite to the shoulder and secure it with a couple of pins on the reference line of the right shoulder (1). Repeat the operation on the left shoulder (2).

To align with the exact point where the knot will be, you need to calculate how many gathers or pleats are needed. (3). Now make a cut at the point where you are going to knot the fabric (4). This cut has two functions: the first helps to calculate the volume of the gather, the second to model the fabric to our liking (following the guidance of the drawing), as we will see below. Now secure the gather with a pin (5).

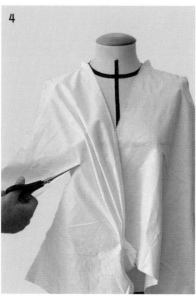

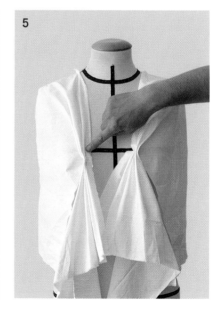

Perform these operations on the left side of the canvas as well: calculate the gather-pleats and cut on the same line until you get the desired width of toile to make them.

Now fit the two pieces of toile together in alignment with their respective cuts.

Hold the toile on the right side (6) and cross it with the left side (7).

Fit the sides together through the gather-pleats cuts (8).

The cut will help us to model the toile as per the drawing and then use or remove the excess toile.

Fold the toile and position it at the desired point (9).

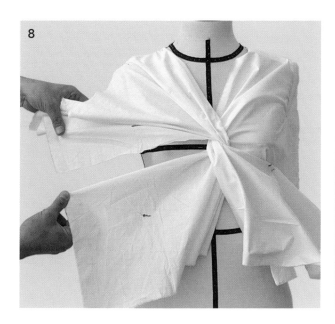

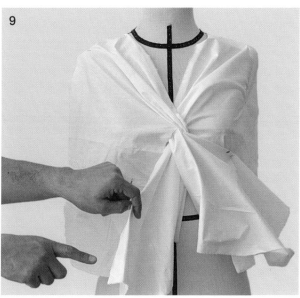

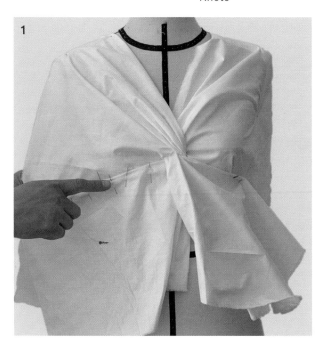

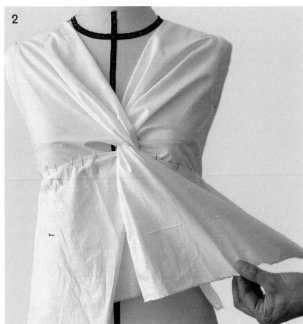

Secure the cut-seam (1) with pins and repeat this operation on the left side.

Now model the part under the bust. Looking at the photo we can see that from the knot emanate pleats-drapes that we are now go-ing to model (2). Remember that, besides the style, we also have to start thinking about the fit and simplifying the model.

So when modelling the toile using pleats-drapes, ensure that you work in a clean way, without letting too much fabric fall under and inside the pleat, so as not to create too much excess waste (3). So keep the idea of style, but simplify from the start and work with precision. Secure your work with pins (4).

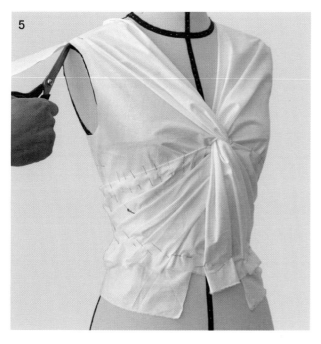

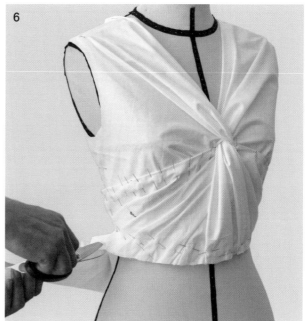

After securing the toile with pins, continue to adjust and trim the excess at the armhole points, at waist level and on the right and left sides (5-6).

The toile is ready to be marked (7-8).

Control points of the model

As we have seen in previous exercises, here too the method for marking the principal points is always the same. Use different colours, make dotted lines, mark the direction of the pleats and write down all the control points (neckline front, shoulder, side, waist, etc.).

Adding letters and numbers will help us later, during the mounting phase, to perform a correct and clear assembly of the model.

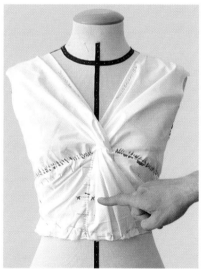 

The reference line where the letter X is placed is a support line that I decided to mark to get more control points. When tailoring the model I can choose whether to sew it or leave it free and secure it only at the waist.

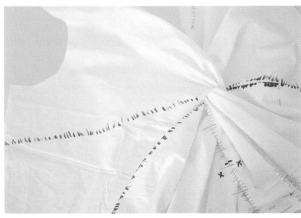

Right side

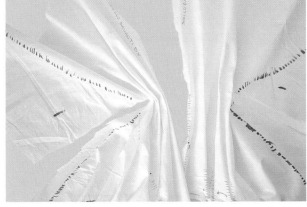

Left side

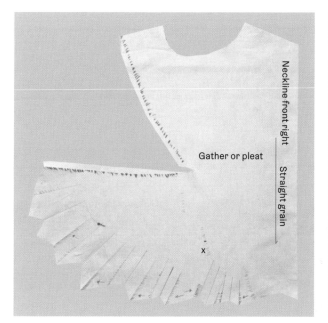

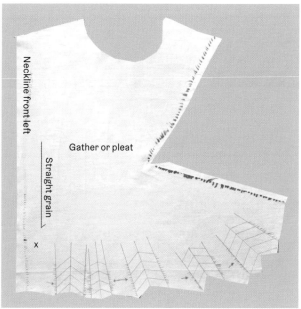

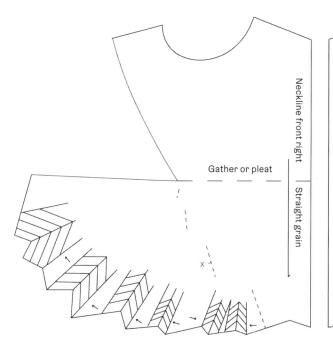

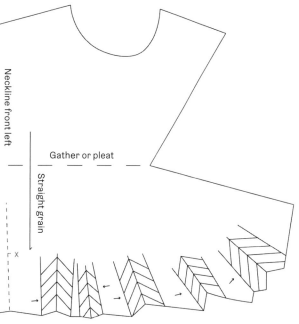

As shown on pg. 90, if we want to get a symmetrical garment we will have to choose the side we like best and duplicate it, so as to work in a mirror-like manner. If instead you want to keep and use the asymmetrical model constructed in this way, you need to correct and align the shoulder seams, the side and the armhole, and the right side with the left.

Collars

Backless dress with high neck at the front

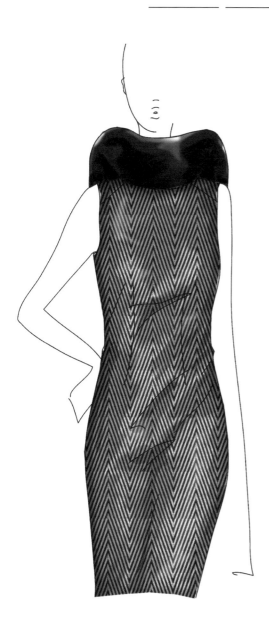

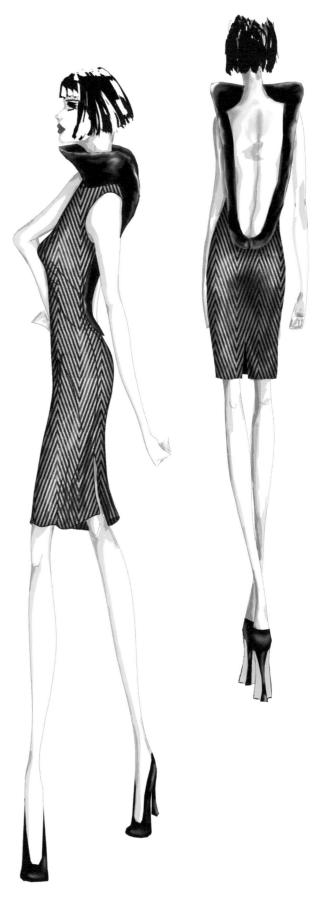

Since this is a symmetrical fitted dress with a wide neckline at the back and a high neck at the front, work in a mirror-like manner, on the 1/2 front and 1/2 back at the same time. For this exercise we can use the base of the sheath dress made earlier.

Since the neck is whole on the front, work it by keeping the centre front on the straight grain, so as bring it back on the other side of the dress.

Preparation of the toile to be modelled

A collar implies a neckline, so to have a clear reference on where the collar will be, you need to position the webbing in the desired position at the base of the dress.

 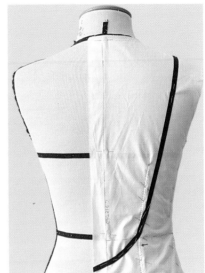

As in the previous exercises, you need to prepare the rectangle to be modelled, the width of which is given by the maximum height of the collar (in this case 14 cm (5.51")) while the length must be equal to the size of the neckline.

Remember to add 2-3 cm (0.78-1.18") to the measurements taken.

Constructing the collar

Fix the rectangle with pins along the line of the webbing marking the neckline. This time, however, the pins should be attached following the direction of the seam and no longer perpendicularly. Since this is a collar, and therefore a volume, positioning the pins perpendicular to the cut would affect toile and create problems.

So, for all collars or volumes, the pins should be positioned following the direction of the seam.

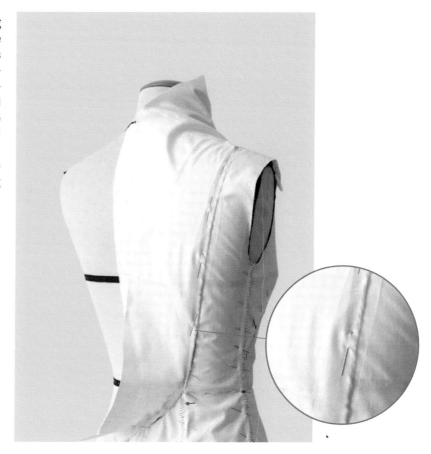

Secure the centre front with a pin. Most likely, having positioned the rectangle on the straight grain on a neckline, therefore on a shape that turns, you will see that the fabric begins to twist and create imperfections. Remember that the fabric has a structure and it will always be the fabric that decides which way to go. So you have to learn how to move the fabric, even if in this case there is very little to move since it has few margins of movement. What follows will be useful for many other steps.

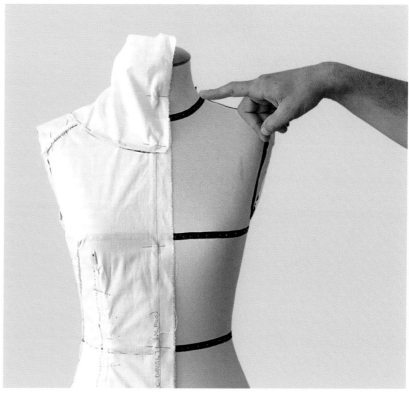

Remember that the fabric has a structure: since this is a stiff toile, the fabric, both in weft and warp, becomes rigid like a piece of wood, while at 45° we find the bias that gives the fabric softness, movement and elasticity. Just think of the petticoat type baby-doll dress in silk that may be worn without an opening (zip, buttons, etc.) because, despite silk being a stiff fabric, if it is cut on the bias the garment feels elasticised. Another example would be the wide shawl collar cut on the bias. To work this collar, however, we are not working on the bias but on the straight grain.

How are we going to solve this problem? What do we need to do to turn the fabric however we want to?

We will make a cut precisely where we want the fabric to turn, rise, fall, open and close. Always make 2 cuts, so as to be able to work the toile in the best way and distribute the opening evenly.

With a cut we will break the rigidity of the straight grain. The cut should be made almost to the end of the fabric, leaving only 2 mm (0.08").

This is one of those instances where Moulage and Modelling must interact. Another example that helps us to better understand this step is the flared skirt made from a sheath dress: just cut from the bottom of the skirt to the waist dart, close the dart and automatically the model will open and turn into a flared skirt (see The decisive cut, pg. 22).

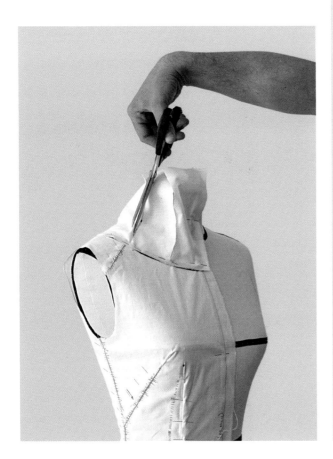

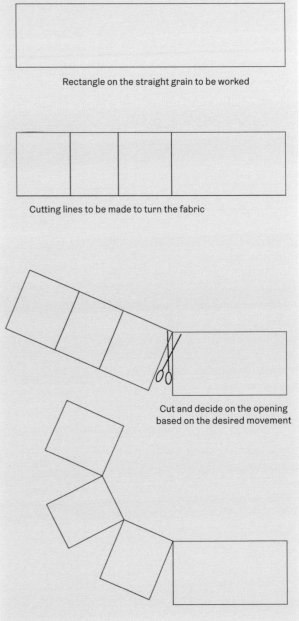

Rectangle on the straight grain to be worked

Cutting lines to be made to turn the fabric

Cut and decide on the opening based on the desired movement

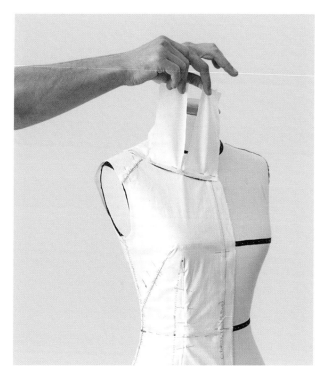
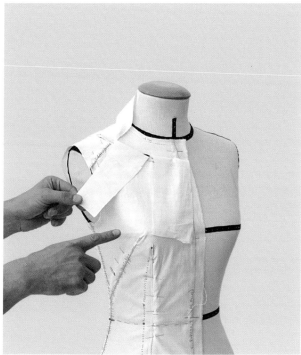

Keep working the collar. After positioning the rectangle cut on the straight grain on the line of the neckline, secure the centre front on the straight grain.

Now make the first and second cut at the exact point where you want the collar to turn. Depending on the desired effect, you can decide how much to open or close the cut. As shown in the images, where the cut was made, the more it is opened, the more the collar will rest on the chest.

After deciding how much to open it, apply a piece of toile where it is missing and join the pieces with some adhesive tape.

This is working with Moulage, deciding how to act at any time and manage the model both in terms of style and modelling.

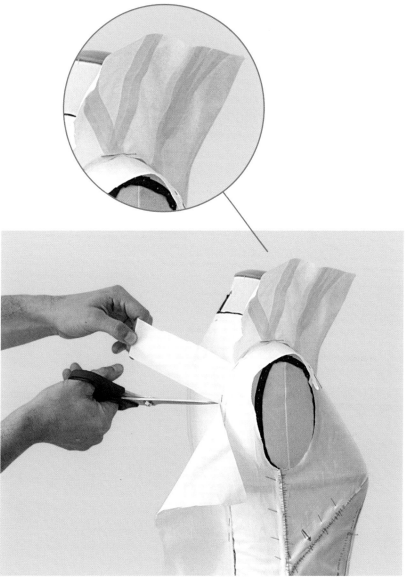

Continue making cuts where you want the toile to move: decide on the opening, take a small piece of toile and we join the pieces with adhesive tape. If while working you realise that you have opened the cut too much, you still have time to close it and modify it how you like.

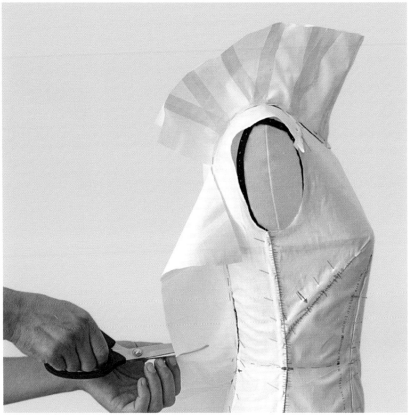

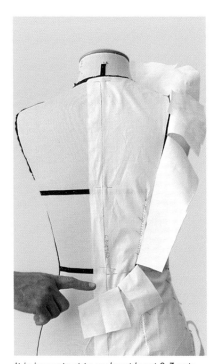

It is important to make at least 2-3 cuts before starting to model the toile.

If you open the cut, the collar will move down towards the dress.

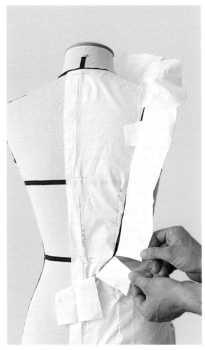

If you close the cut, the collar will rise.

We have seen that, thanks to the cut, we can move the toile as we want. In some cases, since the fabric turns, it may be useful to bring the fabric back onto the straight grain on the centre back, as shown in the photo. For this exercise, it is not of fundamental importance to do so, since the collar will be whole at the front, as already decided.

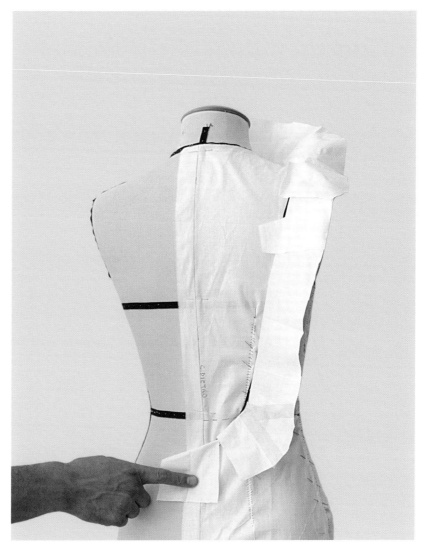

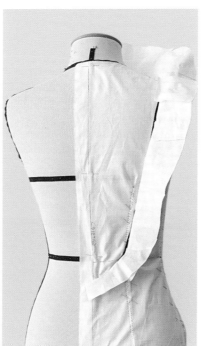

Once the pieces have been joined with adhesive tape, remove the excess fabric. Always use scissors to give the collar the desired shape. Remember that after

disassembling the model you can easily draft the pattern.

Control points of the model

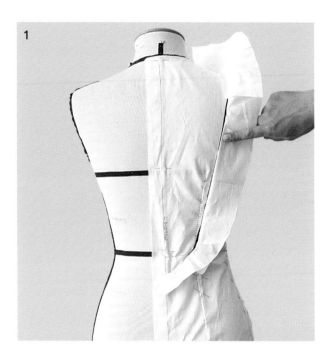

Now we are ready to detect and mark the principal points, but above all to mark the line-cut-seam of the collar and neckline.

Fold back the toile and place it onto the webbing in a natural way (1).

Mark the principal points with a red notch, such as the shoulder, at the points where the model turns and draw a dotted line on the folded toile of the collar which will be the control point of the seam (2).

At the base of the dress, precisely where the webbing is, i.e. on the line of the neckline where the collar will be stitched, mark a dotted line of reference (3).

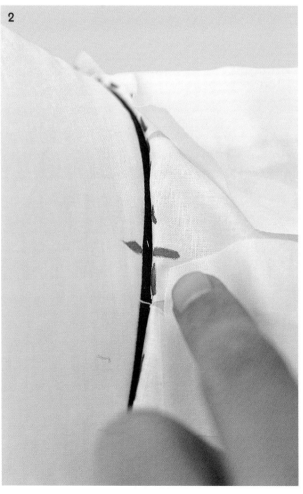

Industrialisation and drafting the pattern of the model

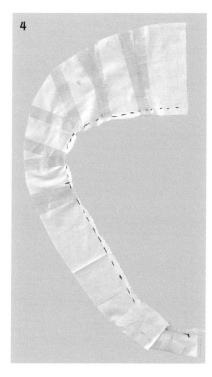

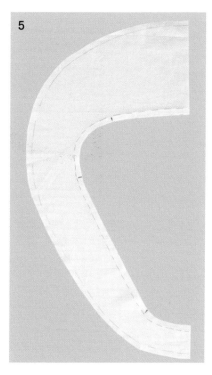

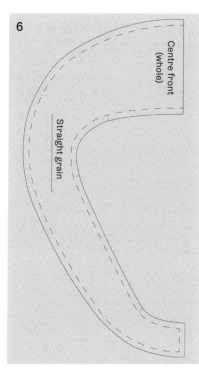

Centre front (whole)

Straight grain

Once the collar has been disassembled and positioned flat, we can adjust it using rulers, set squares and French curves. I recommend removing the seam allowances and cutting exactly at the clearance (4). Put the model back on the toile and make a new model with the corrections made and the seam allowances added (5).

Before putting the model onto paper or inserting it into the Cad, I suggest reassembling it and, if necessary, make the required modifications (6).

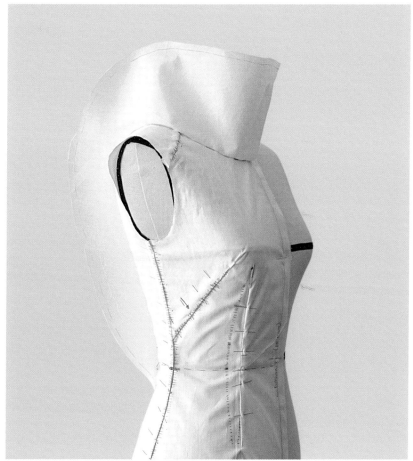

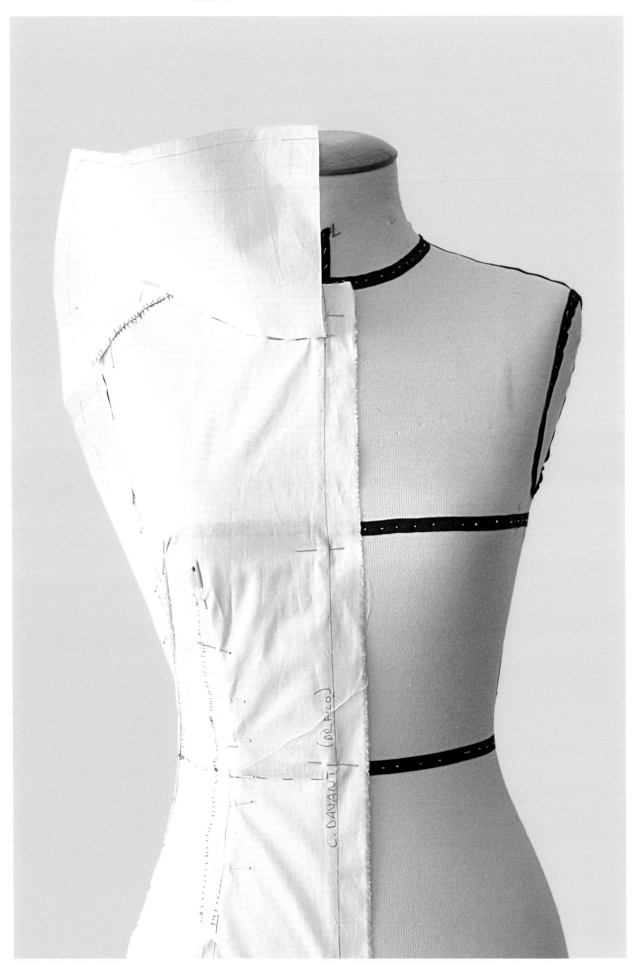

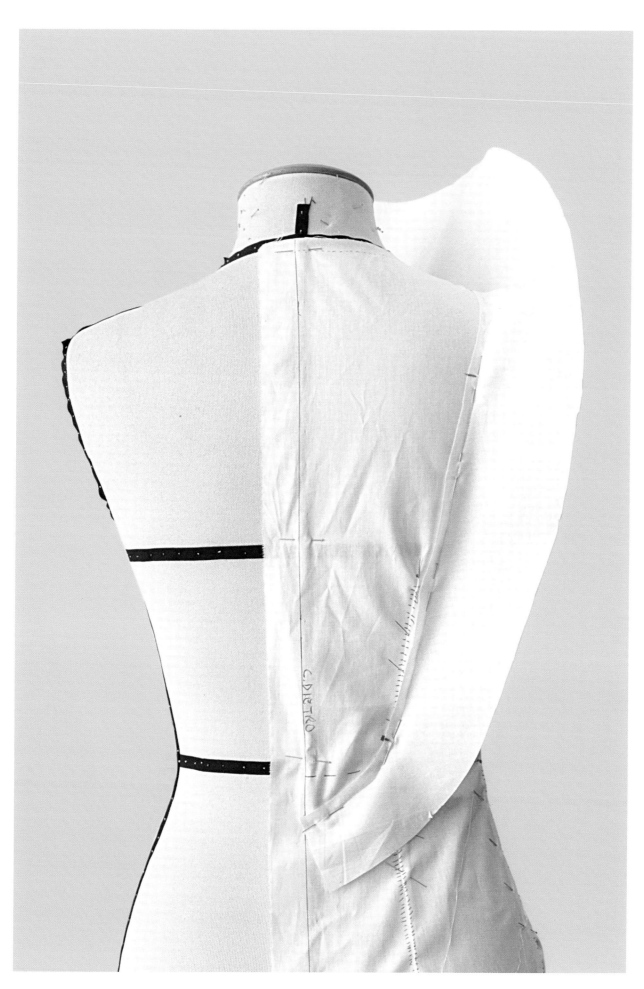

Draping with
volumes

Draped dress with volumes

Do the study of the model.

This dress is short, asymmetrical, characterised by volumes obtained by modelling the fabric with pleats and drapes.

There is a cut at the waist, so first work on the bodice and then the skirt.

Proceed as in the previous exercises, adding to the drawing all the necessary information to understand where to start. Remember that the study of the model is essential, without it you will not know where and how to start.

Preparation of the toile to be modelled

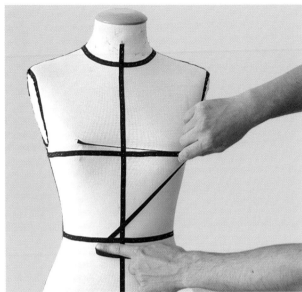

First make the bodice.

From the study of the model you can see that the front of the bodice consists of a large pleat that will help you to obtain a volume. So to calculate how much fabric you need, turn the webbing along the turn of the large pleat, trying to simulate its movement. In this way you will obtain the width of the toile of the bodice front to be modelled.

As for the height, add 10-15 cm (3.93-5.90") more than the measurement that goes from the neckline to the waist cut.

Modelling the bodice with a large pleat-volume

Position the toile on the dress stand in alignment with the line marked on the toile with the webbing of the centre front of the dress stand and secure the toile on the side and the fullest point of the right bust.

Remember that the toile is a set of intertwined threads and you have to find the right thread (exact point of the toile) and make a large pleat downwards.

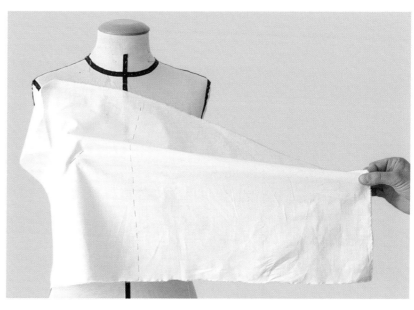

To make the large pleat, put your left hand under the pleat bottom and try to slide the fabric down, making it fit snugly on the body. This large pleat-volume, as well as being an element of style, has the function of giving the right fit to the model since there are no darts or cuts.

Remember that, once you have found the stylistic solution by studying the model and modelling the toile, at the same time you need to think about the fit, the tailoring and where to put the zip or the buttons. Also consider how to make the base-lining, etc. So, we know that apart from creativity there is technique, there-fore in every creation it is important to maintain the concept of style, but, from the start, try to simplify the work to facilitate and make each model feasible.

Continue with the large pleat-volume and secure the toile on the upper part of the left bust.

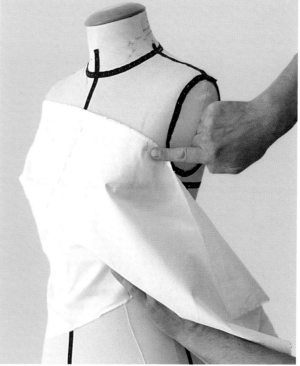

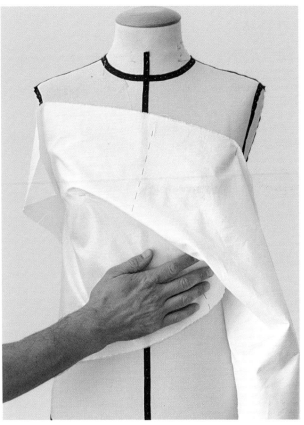

Let the fabric slide down under the pleat bottom.

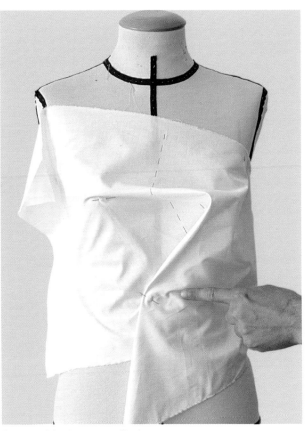

Secure with pins perpendicular to the pleat.

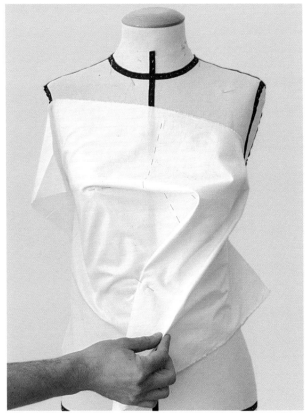

Now make the second pleat, which will help the toile to adhere better to the dress stand, until you get the desired fit.

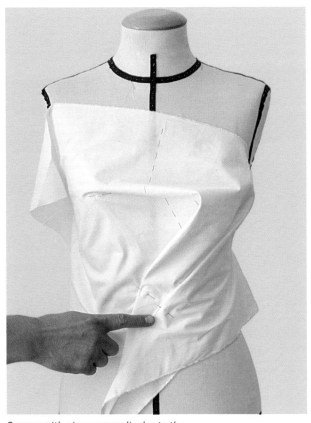

Secure with pins perpendicular to the second pleat.

Start by removing the excess toile below the waist cut, on the sides and on the neckline; use scissors to cut the toile leaving a couple of centimetres for the seams. Remember that if there are curved seams (in this case the neckline) you need to leave 1 cm (0.39") this will help you to work the toile better without creating unwanted ripples, creases or imperfections.

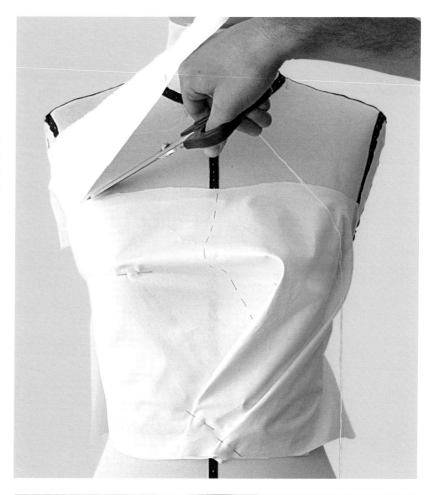

On the neckline of the bodice, fold back the toile on the line of the clearance, so as to already have an idea of how it will be finished and secure the edge with a pin on the centre front. Since this is a volume, the pin will not be attached perpendicularly but following the line of the neckline, so that the volume is not impeded in any way.

After removing the excess fabric, if there are any imperfections, remove the pins, adjust and improve the work until you get the desired effect.

Having finished the bodice front, move on to the bodice back, where the process is exactly the same.

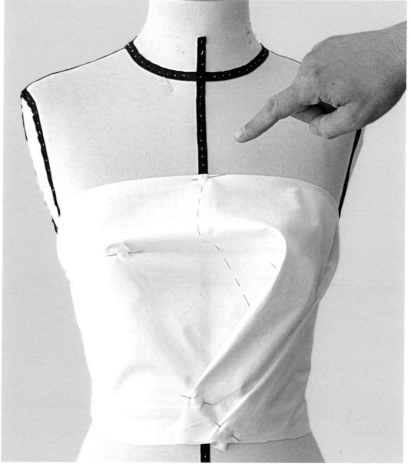

Bodice back

Having a large pleat-volume similar to the bodice front, use the webbing to calculate how much toile to use, just like for the bodice front (1).

Hold the toile at one point, move it and fold it downwards. If the effect of the large pleat-volume is not does satisfactory, try to change the point.

In this case it aligns exactly with the crossing of the warp and the weft, where the bias develops (2).

Slide the fabric under the pleat bottom (3) and finally secure with pins, attached perpendicular to the pleat (4).

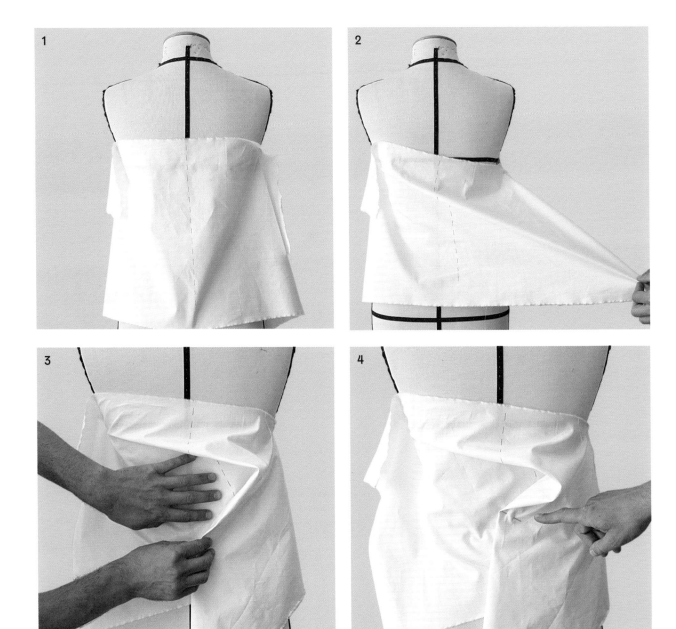

Make the second pleat, which will help the toile to adhere better to the dress stand, until you get the desired fit (5).

Secure with pins attached perpendicular to the pleat (6).

Once you have finished modelling the pleats, remove the excess toile with scissors. Cut the toile leaving a couple of centimetres, which you will need to then add the seam allowances (7).

Fold back the neckline on the line of the clearance and secure the centre back with a pin (8).

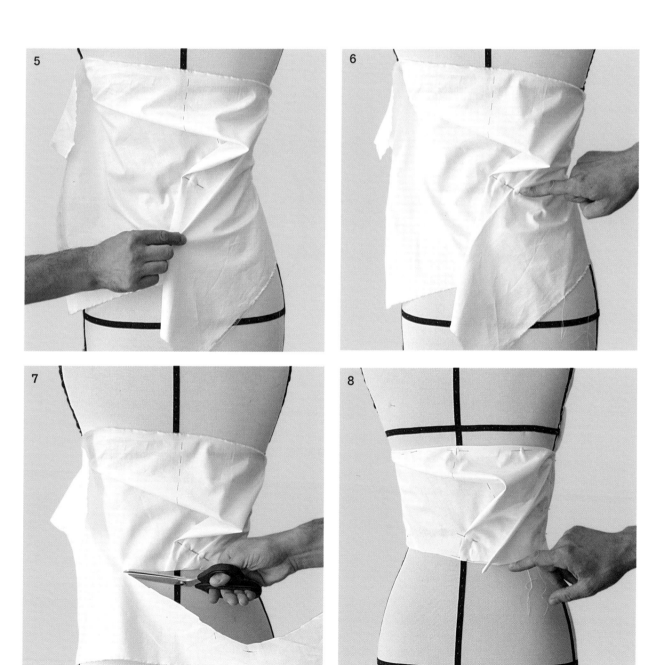

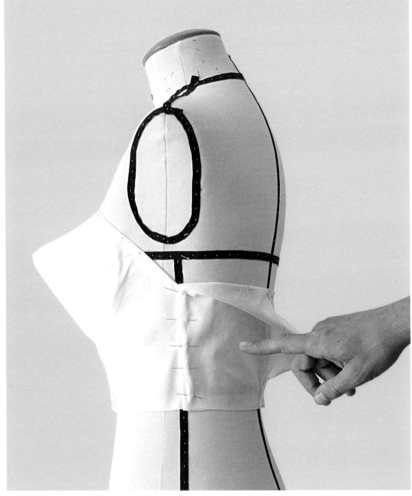

After you have finished modelling the bodice front and the bodice back, join the sides in the same way as for the other models.

Hold the toile on the side back, fold it back and place it on the desired reference line, in this case in alignment with the side webbing.

Securing the side with the pins, inserted perpendicular to the seam, will allow you to adjust the model at any time, to have greater freedom and precision when marking the control points and, as already mentioned, if you are working directly with the final fabric, inserting the pins perpendicular to the seam will allow you to stitch the fabric with a sewing machine with all the pins still attached, thus decreasing the chance of the needle breaking.

Tips

Before going ahead with the skirt, I suggest checking the bodice and the pleats. If you need to adjust the toile at certain points, do not hesi-tate to do so, with the pins inserted externally you can decide to remove them at any time, adjust the toile and secure it again. The model, where possible, should be perfected during the course of the work.

Modelling the skirt

Since we are making an asymmetrical skirt with an opening (zip or buttons) on the left side, modelled with drapes-pleats-volumes, and having use a single piece of fabric, we will make use of the bias. Before starting work, you need to calculate approximately the measurements of the toile to be used: remember that working on the bias involves a greater consumption of toile (often double, but in some cases even more).

Cut a rectangle of fabric with a height (weft width) of 130-140 cm (51.18-55.11") and a base (warp length) of 200 cm (78.74"), and mark a straight line on the exact point of the bias of the fabric. Hold the toile and position the bias on the side line of the dress stand. Pay attention on how to position the toile: as the photo shows, we have to move it upwards until the entire area of the side is covered, that is, up to where the first pleat begins. Secure with pins.

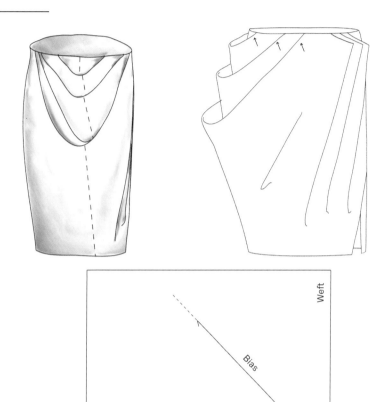

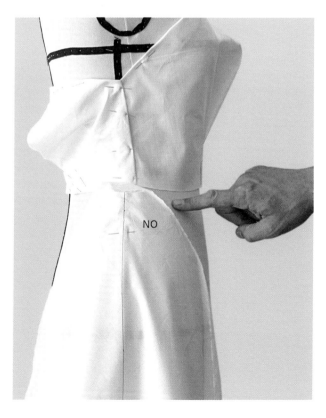

NO

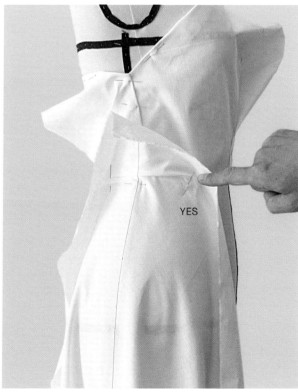

YES

Start modelling the toile: hold the fabric at a point on the front and create a pleat by moving it upwards (1). This step is very important because the pleats can produce different results depending on how we model them. The angle, depth and direction of a pleat are factors that affect the shape, especially in this case, since we will have to successfully obtain volumes from some pleats.

Position the first pleat following the study of the model you made and secure it with pins perpendicularly (2).

Do the same with the back, trying to give continuity to the pleat. Hold the fabric at the exact point where you can obtain a linear and unique pleat-drape running from the front to the back. Then secure with pins (3).

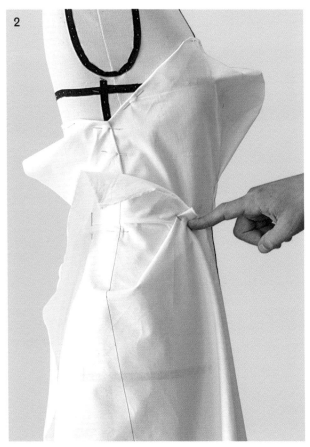

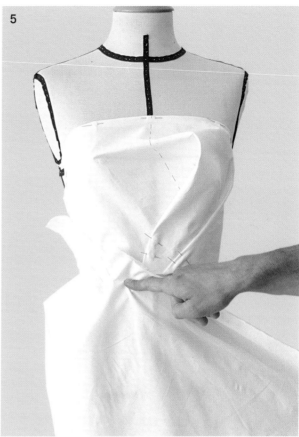

Now hold the toile at a second point to make to the next pleat (4).

Here the depth must be greater so as to be able to give the right volume to the pleat (5).

If the pleat is not satisfactory, undo it and make one with a greater depth (6).

Give the pleat the correct angle, so as to achieve the desired shape (7).

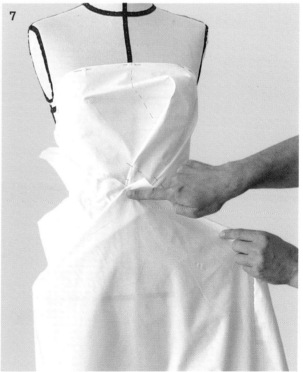

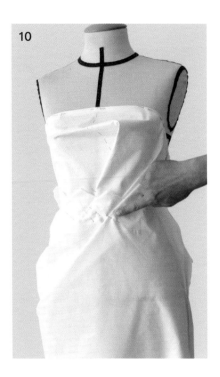

Continue with the back, trying to give continuity to the pleat just created on the front. Then concentrate on modelling both its depth and inclination (8).

Now it's time for the third and last pleat: here the depth will be greater than the second, as the lateral volume you want to obtain is increasing (9).

Having decided on depth and inclination, secure with pins (10) and do the back as for the previous pleats (11).

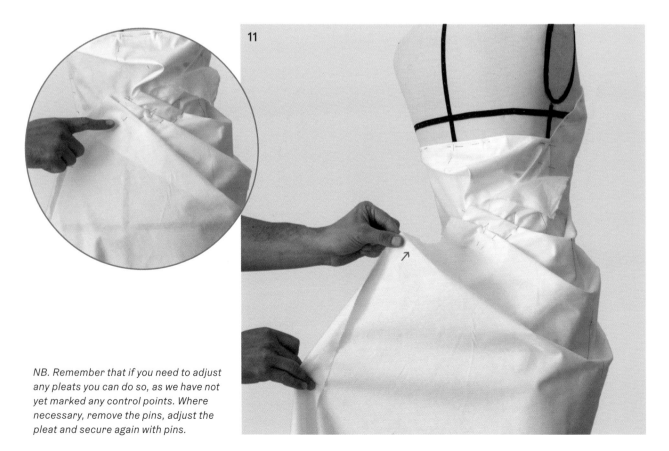

NB. Remember that if you need to adjust any pleats you can do so, as we have not yet marked any control points. Where necessary, remove the pins, adjust the pleat and secure again with pins.

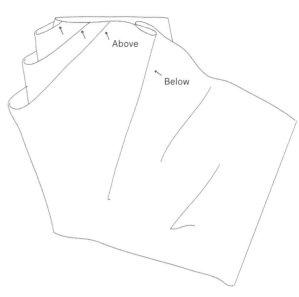

Above

Below

Now let's model the left pleats-ribs (12). This is a different process, but we must still move the fabric in the right direction. I chose this tutorial because I am sure that in the future it will help you to create different types of models.

At the risk of repeating myself, remember that in draping there are no mathematical rules or calculations.

To solve problems related to particular models you have to rely on the fabric and the feeling you get from it. Learning to move the fabric, the commitment, the desire to learn and experience, will enable you to better interpret the movement.

In this case, the depth and inclination we will give to the fabric are fundamental to obtaining the desired

result. Therefore, refer to the images to construct the pleats-ribs (13).

After achieving the desired shape, pin the toile at the two points where it joins (14).

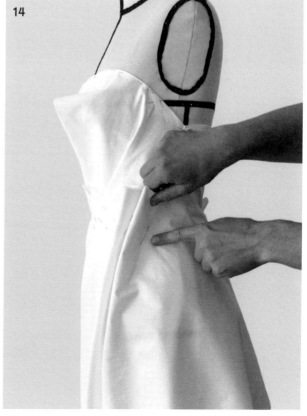

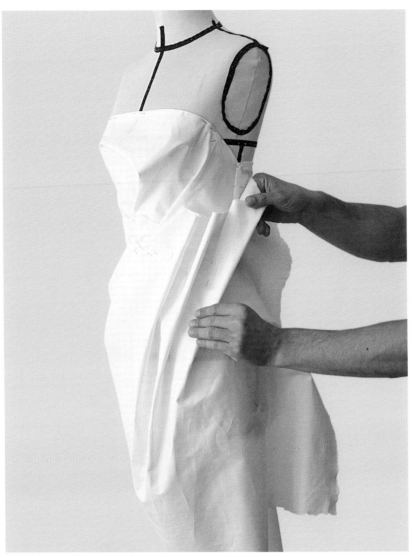

Continue modelling the toile to achieve the desired style. At this point it is important to start simplifying the model and trimming the fabric, to position the toile in the right direction where the side seam will be made.

This step is very important because, when you model the fabric to achieve a certain result, the toile might move unintentionally and lose the position of the straight grain at the point where it was needed.

That said, every time you start to model the toile, in addition to achieving the stylistic result, you also need to think about bringing the fabric back to the right position.

Remove excess fabric.

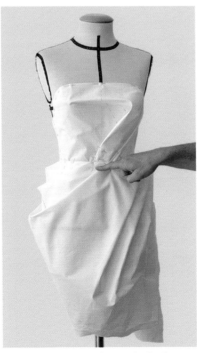

Start attaching the skirt to the bodice.

Fold the toile at waist height, place it on the bodice and secure it with pins.

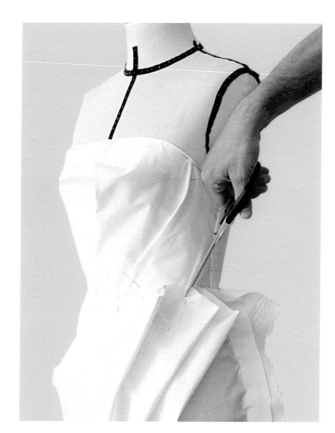

As used when tailoring, if you need to finish off a corner, join different shapes or turn the fabric, the toile requires notching.

Apply this technique here because you need to complete the pleats-ribs and at the same time attach the skirt to the bodice.

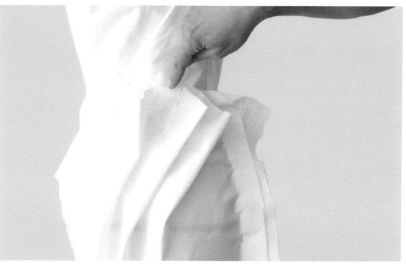

Notch the toile up to where it needs to turn 1 cm (0.39"), fold back the part to be joined to the bodice and secure with pins.

127

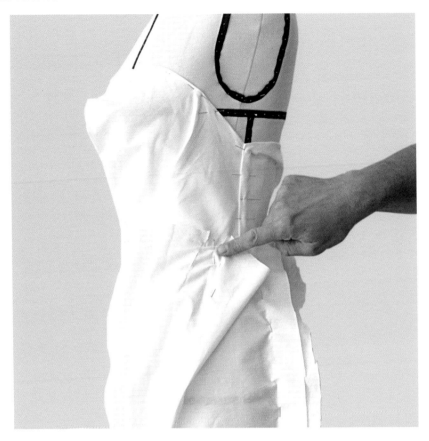

Proceed in the same way for all three pleats-ribs: notch the toile, fold the part to be joined to the bodice and secure with pins.

Now complete the pleat-rib. The notched fabric will help you to accomplish this step.

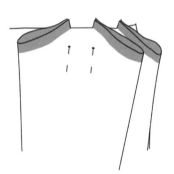

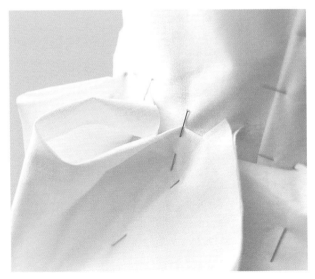

Cut off the excess toile leaving the seam allowance and fold the toile inside.

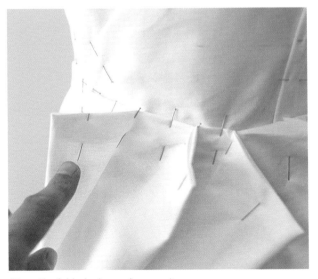

Close the folded edge and secure it with pins.

To complete the model, finish off the left side, then remove the excess fabric.

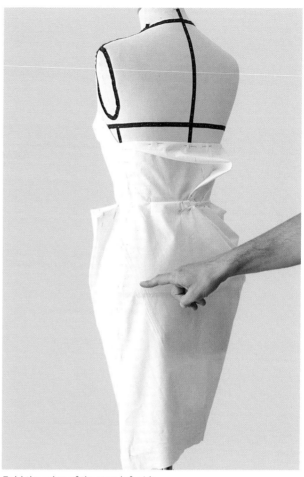

Fold the edge of the rear left side toile and place it on the front toile at the webbing.

Attach the pins perpendicularly to secure the side seam and the edge of the side slit.

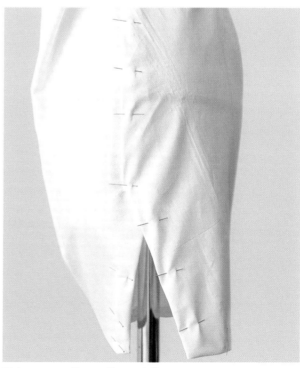

Make a general inspection and, if necessary, adjust a few details, and do not hesitate to remove the pins.

Control points of the model

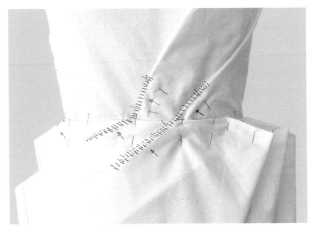

Mark the pleats with red dotted lines.

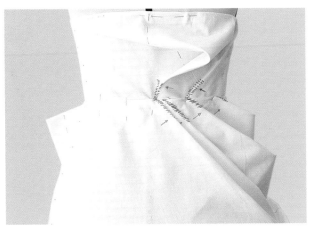

Mark the direction of the pleats.

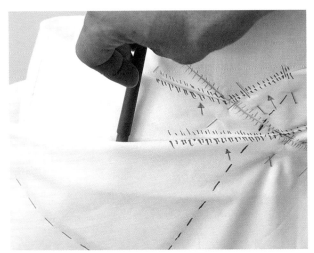

Mark the inside of the pleat bottom with a continuous line.

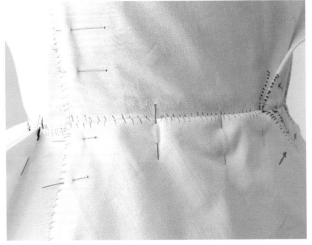

Use black dotted lines to mark all the seams: side, waist, etc.

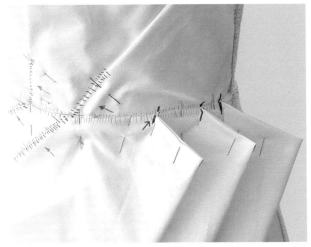

With a red dotted line-notch mark the outside of the pleats-ribs.

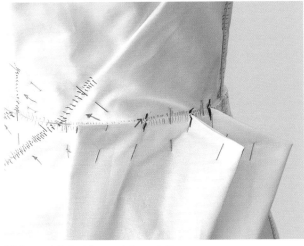

With a red dotted line-notch mark the outside of the pleats-ribs.

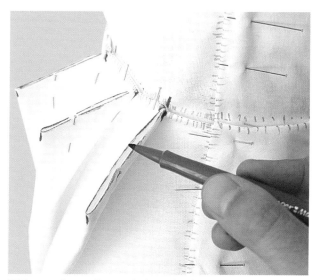

With a continuous line mark the ends of the pleats-ribs which will be joined with a seam during construction.

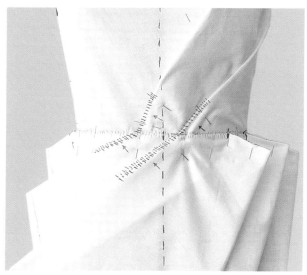

Mark the centre front and centre back with a red dotted line.

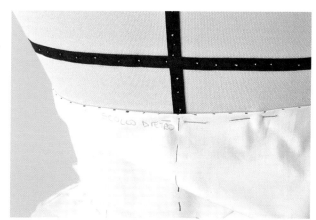

Mark the neckline front and the neckline back with dots.

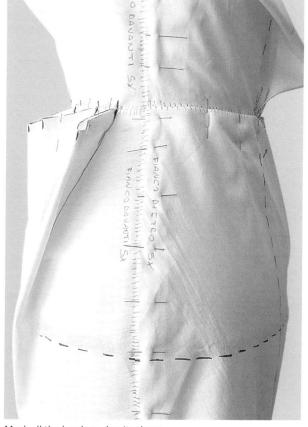

Mark all the levels and write down all the control points: right and left side front and side back, neckline front, neckline back, hem, etc.

Industrialisation and drafting the pattern of the model

Having marked all the control points of the model, you can remove it from the dress stand.

Before removing all the pins and drafting the pattern, open the side where the opening will be (zip or buttons) and check the inside to see if there are points to adjust, pieces of toile to add or remove. I always recommend first working one piece and then the other, so first the bodice and then the skirt.

BODICE FRONT

The image below shows the inside of the bodice front; as you can see the fabric of the pleat bottom needs adjusting. You can add some toile or decide to close the hole of the pleat bottom. In this case I suggest removing some fabric and closing the pleat bottom with a seam.

Consequently, you will use less fabric, but above all, not having added more toile up to the waist seam (where there are also the pleats of the skirt), you will avoid having an accumulation of fabric, which helps the tailoring and the look of the garment.

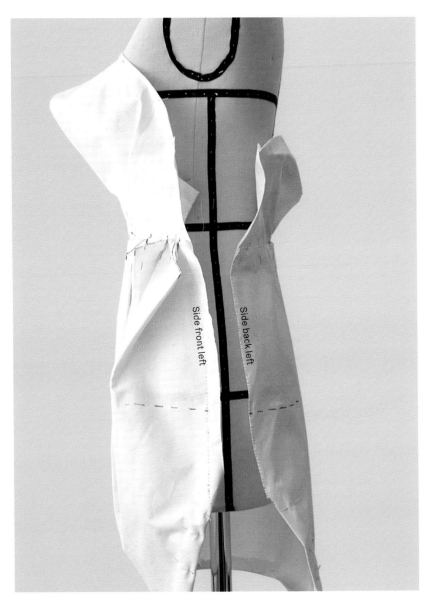

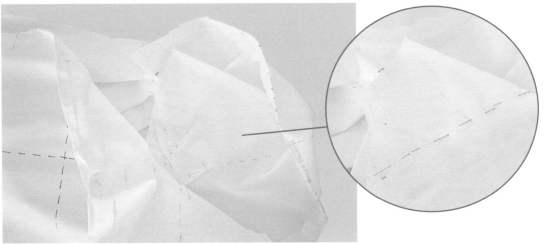

134

*Remove the excess toile 1 cm (0.39")
from the pins.*

*Mark the control points using a letter or
number to facilitate assembly.*

Side front right

In this case, having pleats and
drapes, before opening the model
to continue to improve it, you need
to remove the excess toile leaving
1 cm (0.39") for the seam allowance.
By cutting with the pleats closed,
when you open the model you will
have the right pleat shape with the
allowance already added.

BODICE BACK

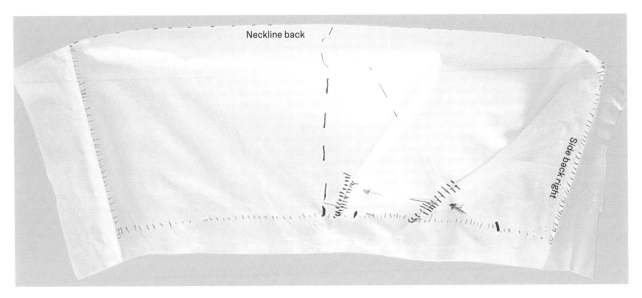

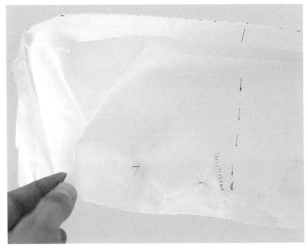

Check the bodice inside: pleat bottom, seams or for imperfections (e.g. unwanted creases or ripples).

The pleat bottom goes up to the waist seam, so leave it that way. If you want to remove some toile to streamline the model, proceed as for the front.

So, before you draft the pattern of the model, you need to remove the excess toile in the waist seam. Remember to cut with the pleats still closed, leaving 1 cm (0.39") for the seam allowance.

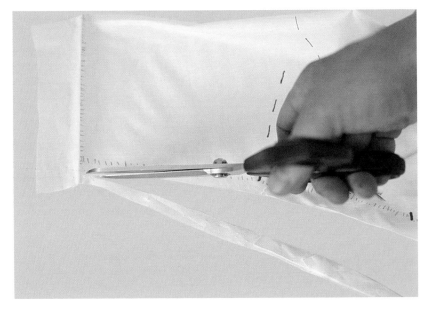

DRAFTING THE PATTERN OF THE BODICE FRONT

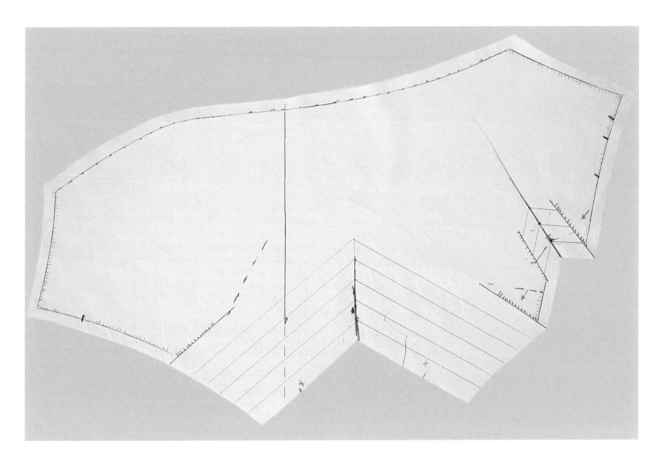

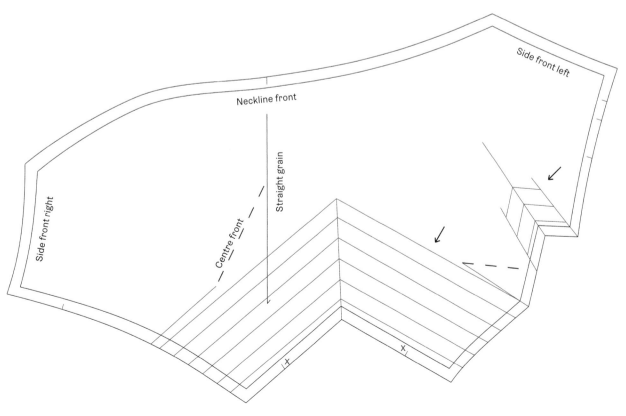

Side front left

Neckline front

Straight grain

Side front right

Centre front

Side front right

DRAFTING THE PATTERN OF THE BODICE BACK

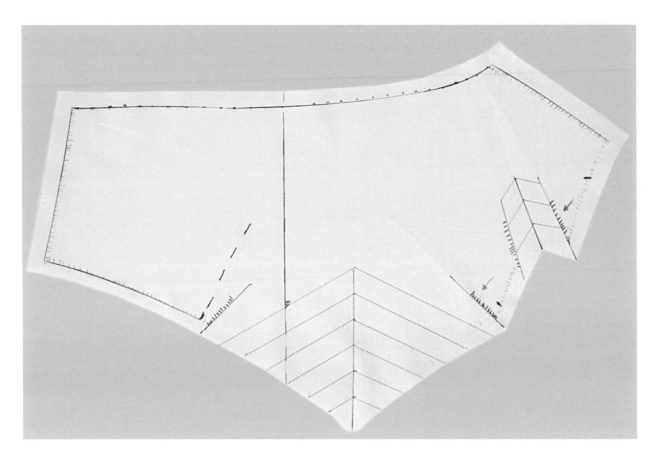

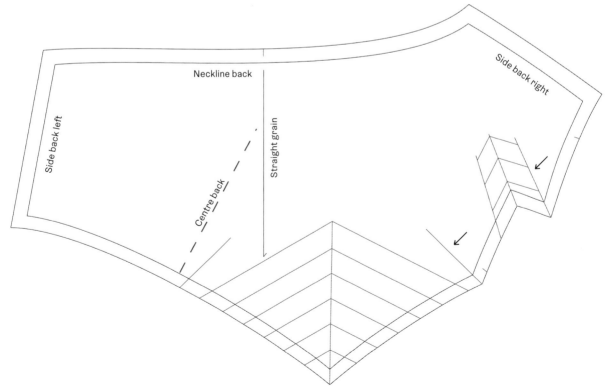

Neckline back

Side back left

Side back right

Centre back

Straight grain

DRAFTING THE PATTERN OF THE SKIRT

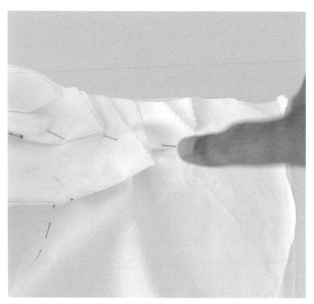

Check the inside of the skirt as for the bodice. Again, some pleats need more toile.

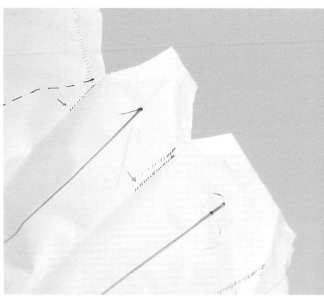

Open the model and decide whether to add toile or close the pleat bottom with a seam (as done on the bodice). In this case we will add a piece of toile.

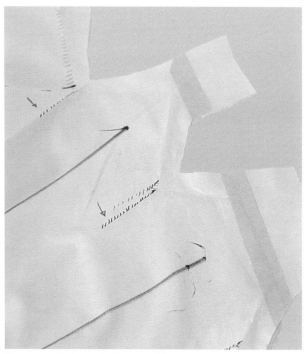

Take a small piece of toile and add it to the model with adhesive tape.

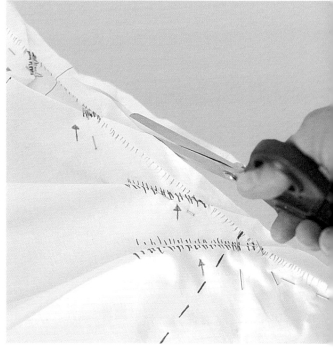

Close the pleats and remove the excess fabric adding 1 cm (0.39") to the clearance for the seam allowance.

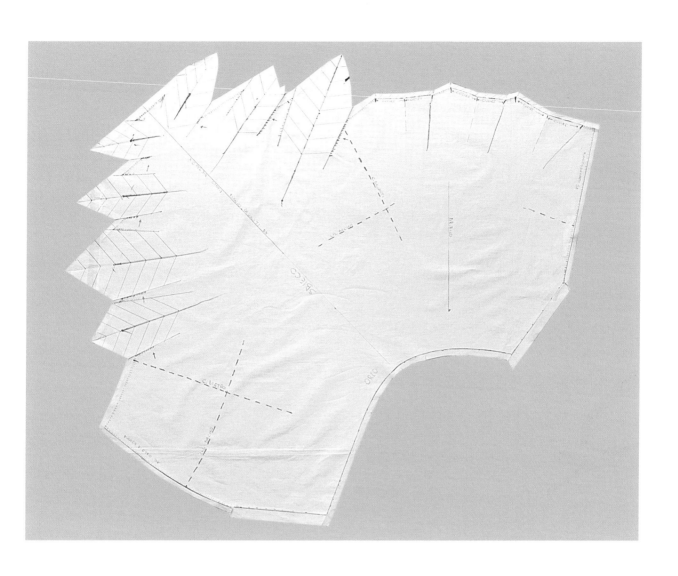

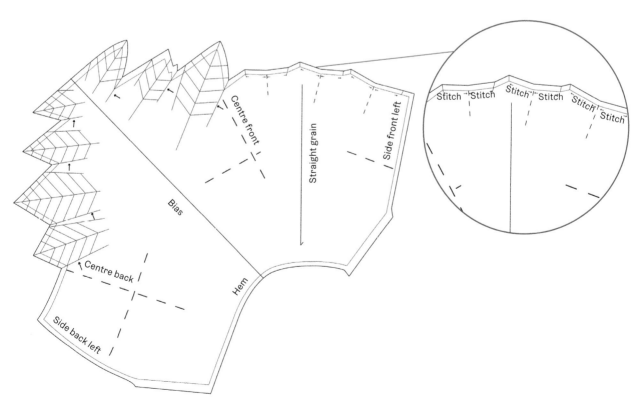

Centre front

Straight grain

Side front left

Bias

Centre back

Hem

Side back left

Stitch Stitch Stitch Stitch Stitch Stitch

Bodice
with volumes

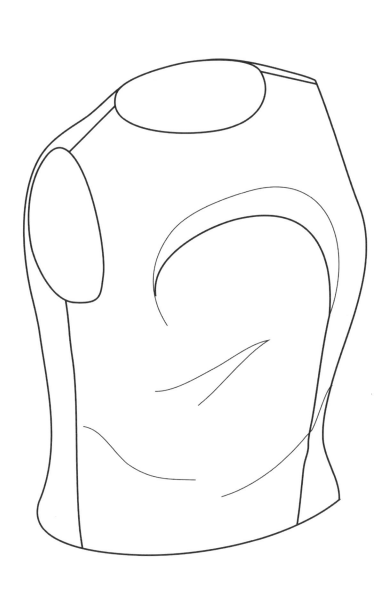

Before starting to model the canvas you need to understand how to operate. Proceed as in the previous exercises, adding to the drawing all the necessary information to understand where to start.

Since this is an apparently uncomplicated bodice with a volume, you should work on a simple base, add a bezel cut on the bias where you want to obtain the volume and make the changes.

Preparation and modelling of the toile

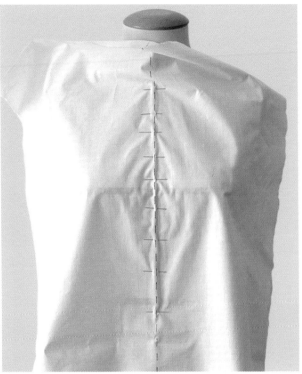

Mark the centre front exactly in the middle of the toile, respecting and following the direction of the straight grain and secure with pins.

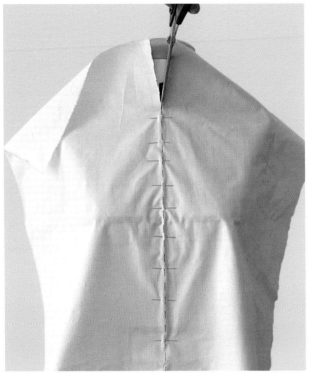

Remove the excess toile: make a cut on the line of the centre front up to the line of the neck.

Mark the neck on the toile with a pencil, remove the excess toile and secure the toile on the chest with the pins.

Tips

The study of the model is very important for a precise and fast design. Understanding where to start and how to proceed, will give you an immediate idea of how to model the toile. If there are any areas where the toile appears stiff, solid and clean, it will almost certainly be positioned on the straight grain at that point.

For this reason we have chosen to start positioning the toile on the straight grain.

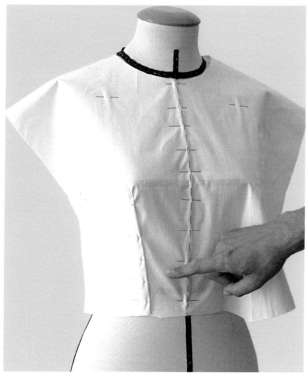

Model the toile by making a dart on the right side until the desired fit is achieved.

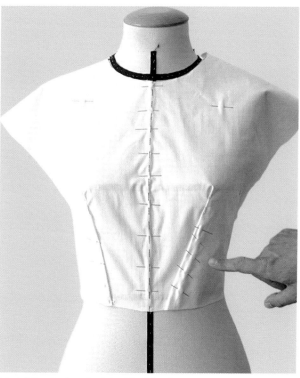

Model the dart on the left side following the angle shown in the drawing and secure with the pins perpendicularly.

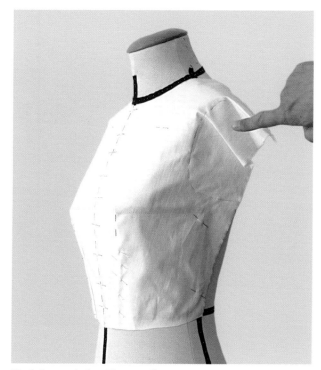

Mark the armhole with a pencil respecting the control points.

Remove the excess fabric by cutting exactly on the mark shown.

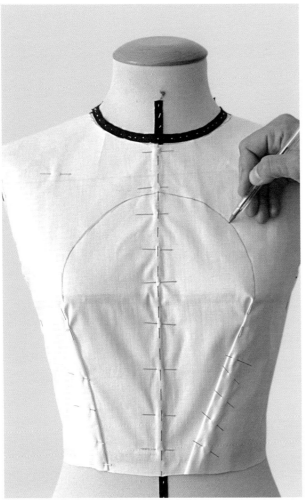

Mark the reference line on the bodice
base where the volume will go.

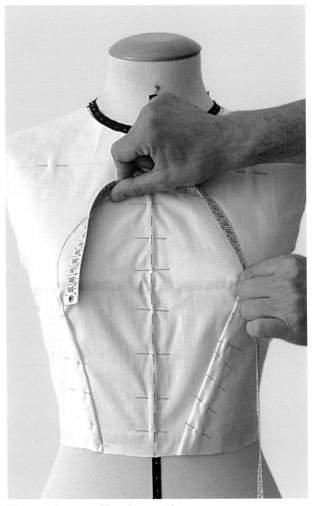

Measure the curved line drawn with a
tape measure, going from the fullest
point of the right bust to the fullest point
of the left bust.

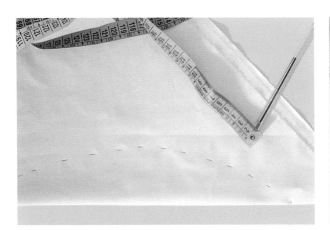

Take a new toile and fold it exactly in two
on the line of the bias. Draw a bezel near
the fold of the same size previously done
on the base of the bodice.

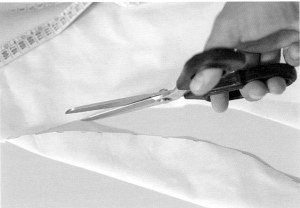

Cut the bezel on the curved line drawn.

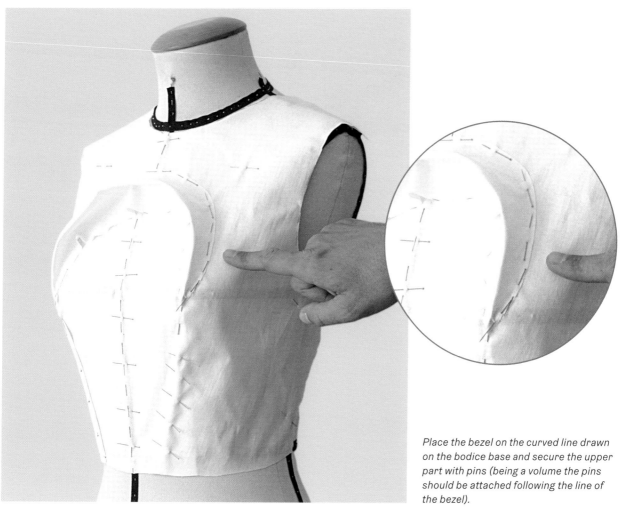

Place the bezel on the curved line drawn on the bodice base and secure the upper part with pins (being a volume the pins should be attached following the line of the bezel).

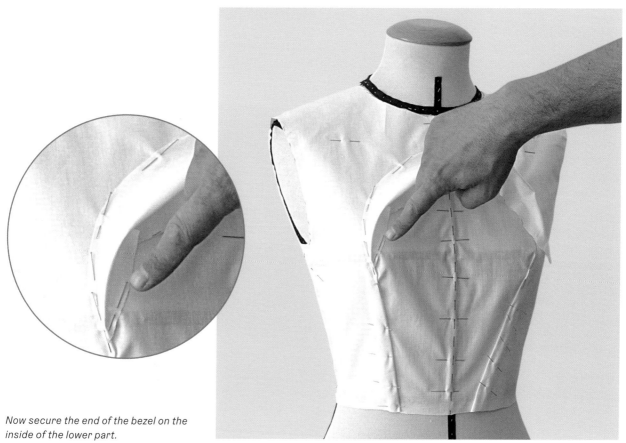

Now secure the end of the bezel on the inside of the lower part.

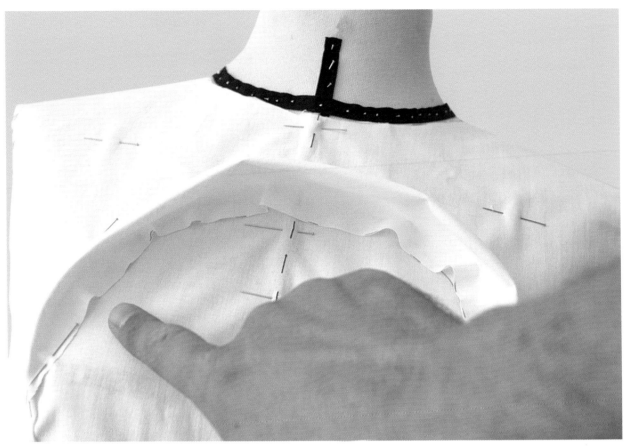

Now you need to join the bezel to the bodice base with adhesive tape, trying to eliminate as naturally as possible the ripples visible in the photo.

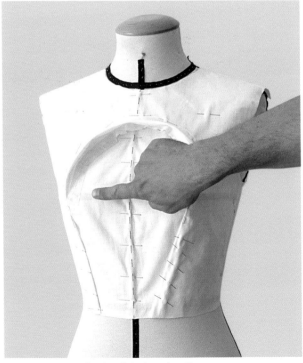

Tape starting at the tip of the bezel on the right side.

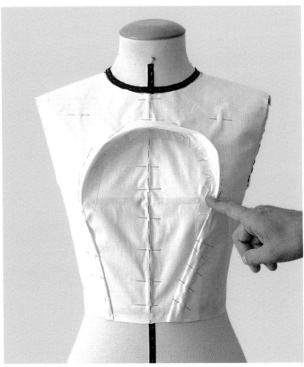

Tape the entire lower part of the bezel.

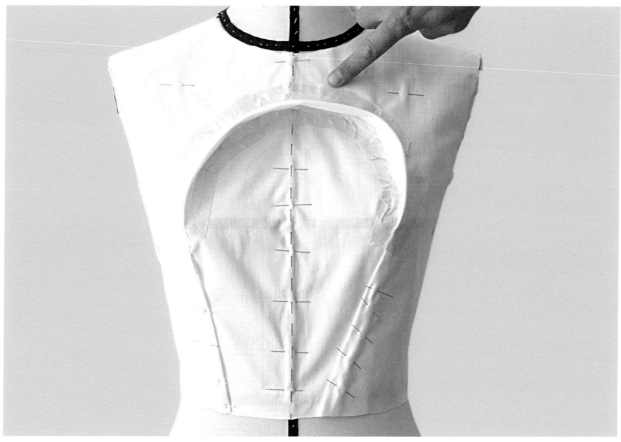

Then tape the upper part of the bezel to the bodice base.

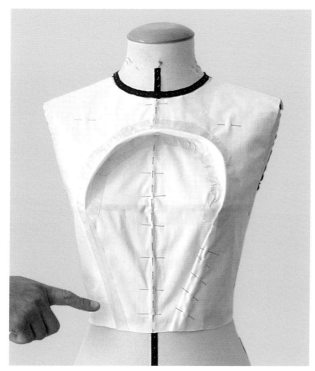

Having to make the bodice front with a volume in a single piece, you need to remove the right dart, so again use adhesive tape to close the dart.

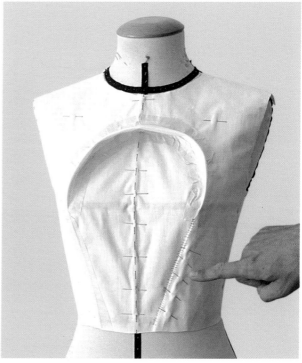

Mark the left dart with dotted lines.

Bodice with volumes

Mark the bust level with a red dotted line.

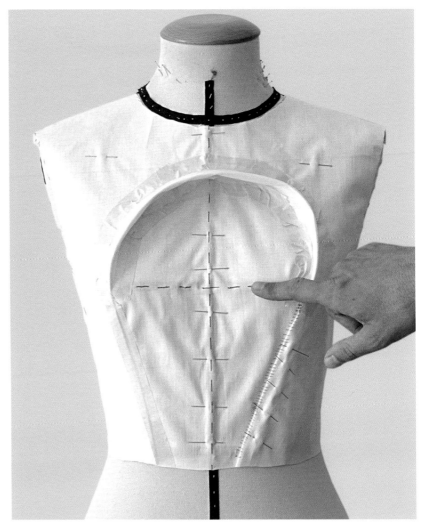

Now remove the bodice from the dress stand to make the changes.

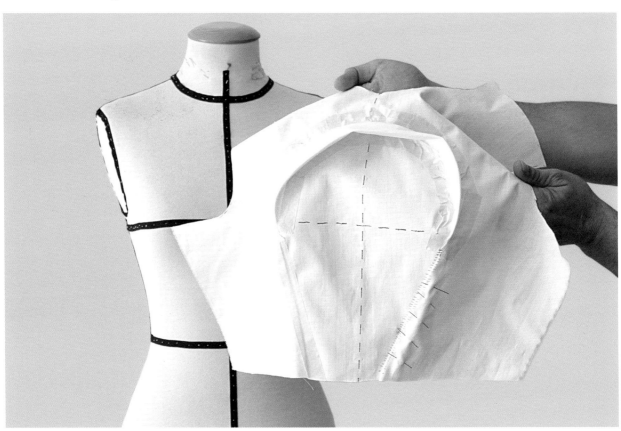

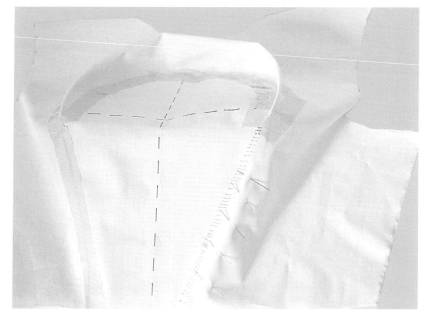

From the study of the model you can see that the bodice is made of a single piece of fabric on the front, with a single dart, whose function is not just to make a good fit but, above all, to create the volume.

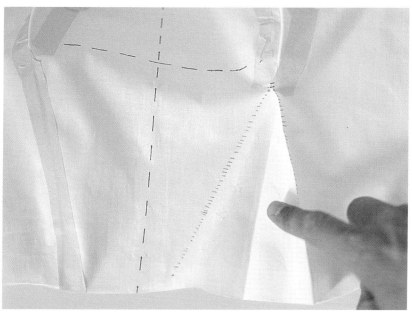

Remove the pins from the left side dart and open it.

Make a cut from the bottom (start of the dart) upwards (end of the dart).

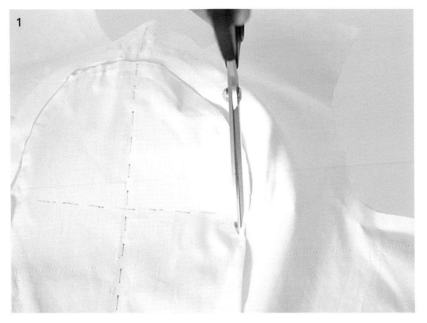

Turn the model over and continue to cut, following the line made on the bodice at the beginning, exactly in line with the centre of the applied bezel, to the opposite end, at the fullest point of the right side bust, where the tip of the bezel (1) rests.

Turn the model over again and make a cut in the lower part of the bezel, precisely where you made the join (bodice and bezel) with the adhesive tape (2-3).

Now let's say that the bodice base is flat, except for the volume of the bezel you just added. At this point you need to make a further change to obtain a totally flat shape, namely the paper pattern.

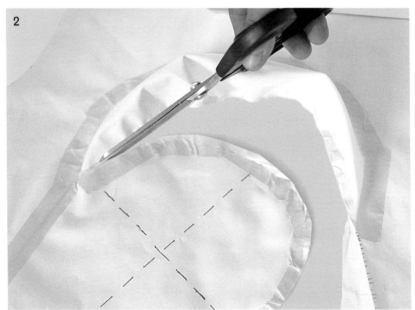

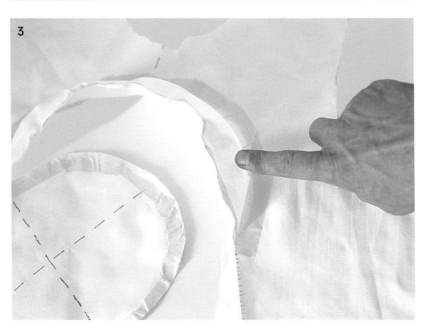

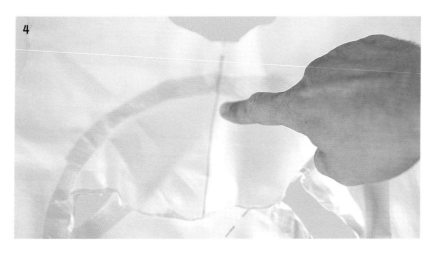

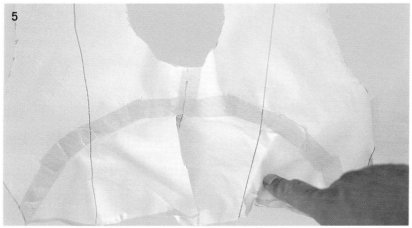

Mark the centre of the bezel with a red pen and cut only the bezel, without touching the bodice base (4).

Mark and cut along the red line from the bezel to the right centre shoulder and left centre shoulder. In this case, remember that the cut must be made to the end leaving only 2 mm (0.08") of the toile intact (5).

Mark a line from the end of the bust to the armhole, both on the right and left side (6).

Cut along the line to the end and leave 2 mm (0.08") (7).

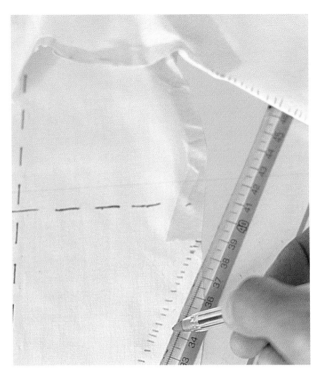

Cut along the line leaving the seam allowance.

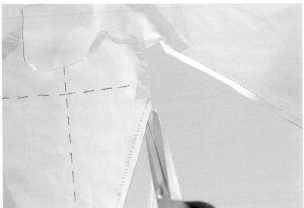

Now give the dart the right allowance. Since this is a dart that will result in a curve, in this case I recommend leaving 0.7 cm (0.27") for the seams and stitch at 0.5 cm (0.19"); this will allow the fabric to turn well without too much forcing.

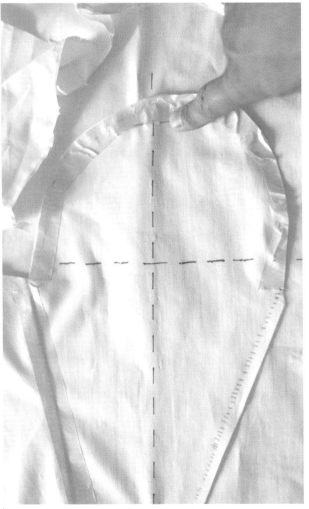

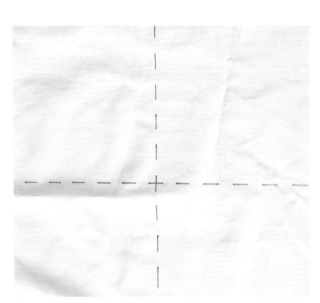

Now more accurately redraw the model with the changes made. Take a new piece of toile, mark the centre front and bust level.

Place the model on the toile in alignment with the control points detected and secure with pins.

Measure the bodice cut-dart line with a tape measure and redraw the other bezel cut-dart line with the same measurement. Thanks to the cuts made previously, you can open up until you get to the right size.

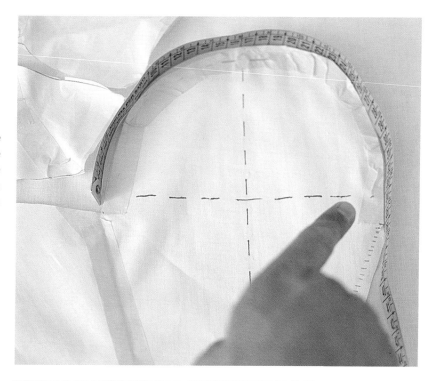

In the cut made at the centre of the bezel (leaving the bodice base whole) you can see that the two edges of toile overlap and, for this reason, we will lose 4-5 cm (1.57-1.96"), which, as we will see below, will be recovered by opening more cuts made in the right and left armholes. On the other hand, the cut on the right and left shoulder should be opened until the two ends-corners of the bezel touch each other.

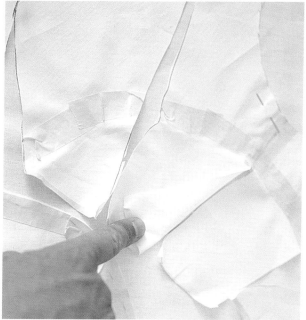

Then proceed as follows: allow the edges of the toile to overlap in the cut at the centre of the bezel; open the shoulder cuts until the two ends-corners of the bezel touch each other. Make sure that the model flattens naturally without too much forcing.

Bodice with volumes

Now the opening of the cut in the
armhole will allow us to achieve the
desired size.

Cut and open. Try to distribute the
opening of the cuts equally in the right
and left armholes.

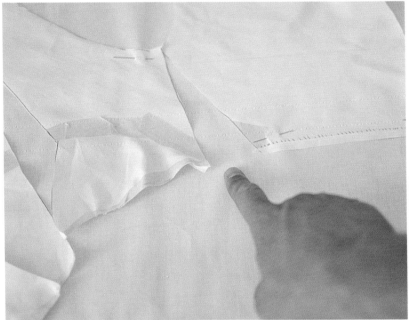

Use a tape measure to check if the
measurements match.

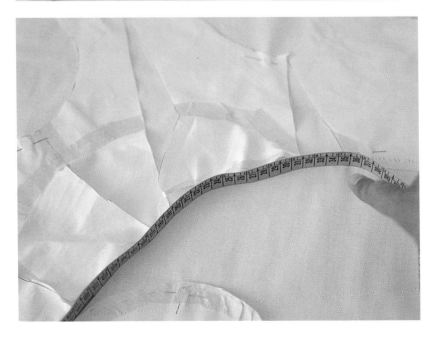

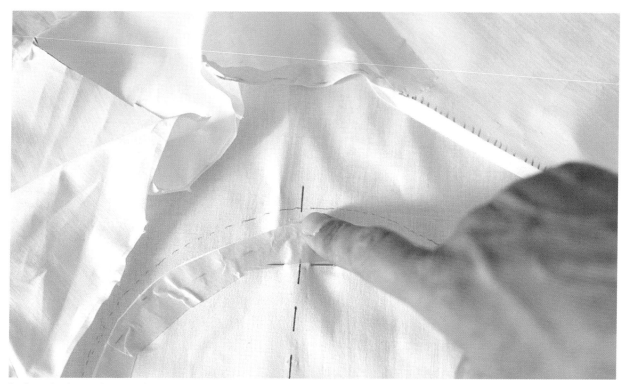

Redraw the dart with a French curve and remember to add the seam allowances. Finally, cut respecting the control points shown.

The model is ready to be mounted and tested again on the dress stand, so you can make further improvements.

Redraw the same shape and position of the armhole on both sides and remark, where necessary, all control points, such as side seams, shoulder seams, waist level, bust level, etc.

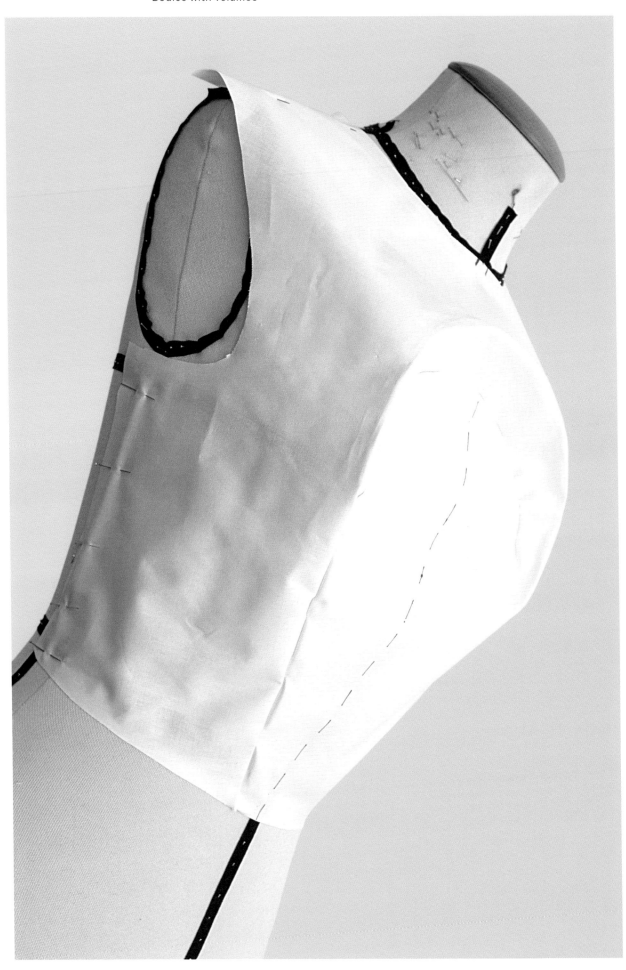

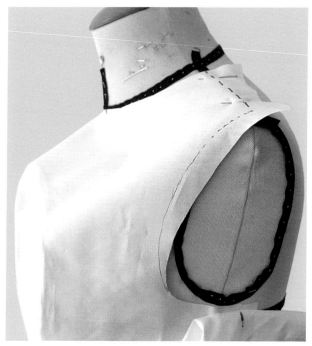

After you have centered and positioned the model, correct and draw with a red pen the desired armhole.

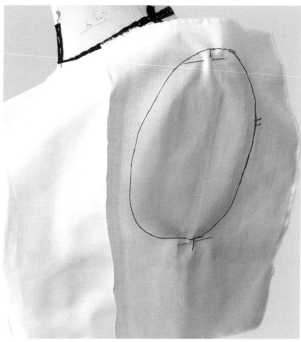

Take a rectangular piece of toile and secure it with pins copying the shape of the armhole underneath. Add reference notches on the shoulder seam and side seam, as well as two notches to indicate the back.

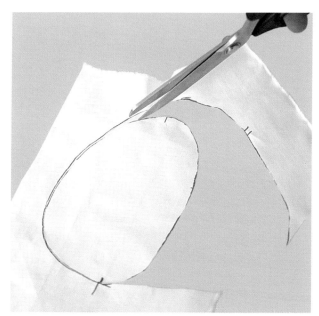

Lay flat and cut out the exact shape.

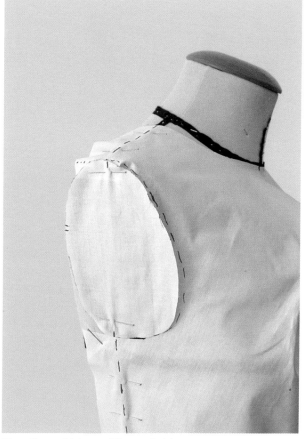

Place the oval (shape of the armhole) on the right side and re-mark the armhole.

Mark the shoulder control point with a dotted line.

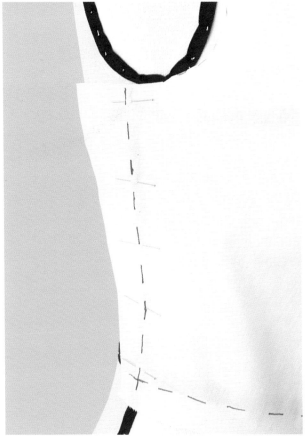

Mark the hip line and waist line.

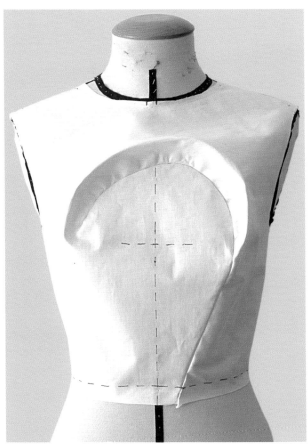

The model is ready to be disassembled and put onto paper.

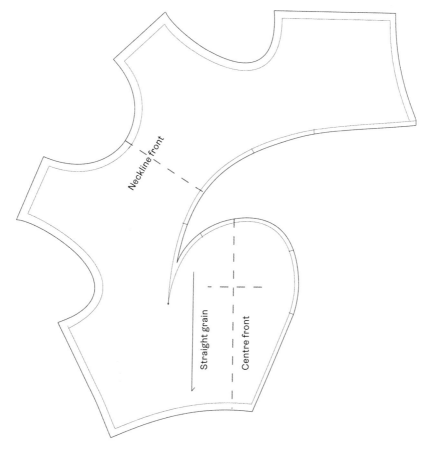

Neckline front

Straight grain

Centre front

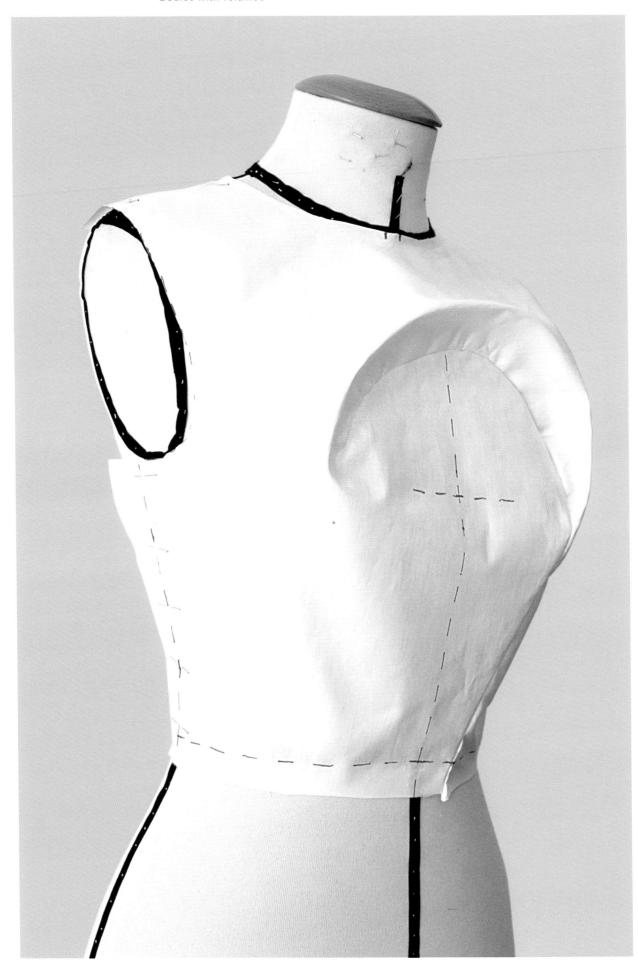

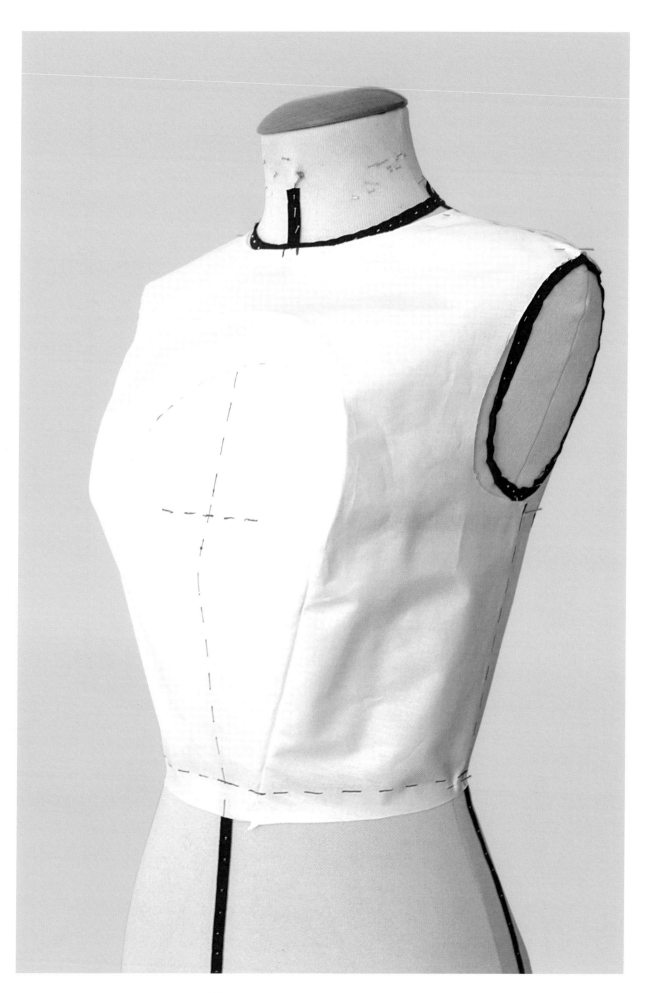

Basic
sleeve

The term sleeve encompasses countless types. Here I will explain just the basic construction of a size 40-42 EU / 12-14 UK.

There are several factors that affect the shape, angle and position of the sleeve. The first is the type of clothing on which it will be applied: it could be sporty, casual, classic, etc. This will determine the fit.

For a classic garment you definitely need a straight sleeve, namely with a minimal angle. For a casual or sporty garment, the sleeve angle will be greater, so the height of the cap-trumpet of the sleeve and its width will also change relative to this. You can check this by comparing the clothes in your wardrobe and seeing the difference. An example is shown below.

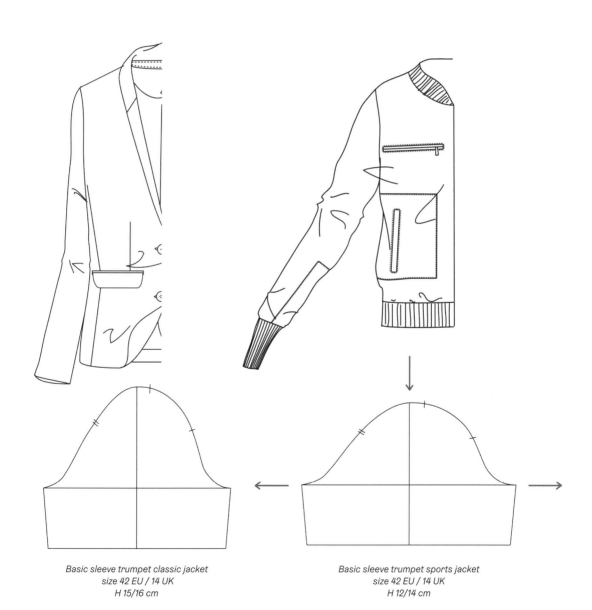

Basic sleeve trumpet classic jacket
size 42 EU / 14 UK
H 15/16 cm

Basic sleeve trumpet sports jacket
size 42 EU / 14 UK
H 12/14 cm

Preparation of the toile to be modelled

As in the previous exercises, again you have to prepare the rectangle of toile to be modelled. These and other measurements are available in the various tables on the market, but here we will simply respect their control points, but as we will see, these measurements can also be taken directly on the person. So, the width of the sleeve corresponds to the width of the bicep plus the degree of fit (32+2 cm) (12+0.78"), while the length of the sleeve will be determined by the length measured on the person, adding 5-8 cm (1.96-3.14") more (61+8 cm) (24.01+3.14").

Proceed by locating point D (the start of the armpit-armhole level). From this point we can determine the height of the sleeve cap-trumpet to be perfected during modelling. In this case, point C will be determined later, after the sleeve has been modelled. Consequently, point D (hypothetical cap height + 3-4 cm (0.39-1.57") more for modelling later) will be positioned at least 20 cm (7.87") from point X.

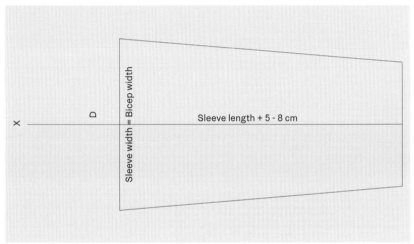

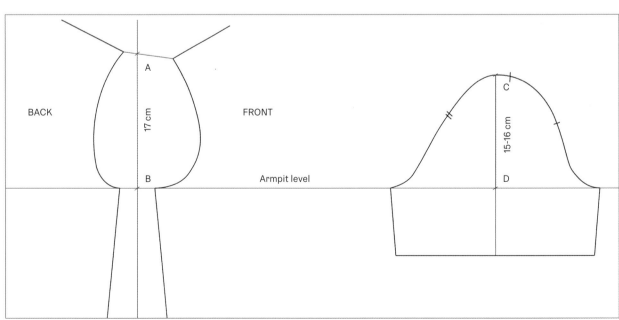

A-B = 17 cm (variable measurement) *C-D = 15-16 cm (variable measurement)*

Now mark on the toile to be modelled an outline of the armhole to obtain control points on how and where to position the sleeve and to remove the excess toile.

We can proceed in two ways: the first involves placing the toile of the sleeve on the bodice front and on the bodice back, balancing them and then copying their respective armholes (1).

The second method, on the other hand, involves marking approximate control points (remember that the sleeve is going to be modelled and only then will we identify the exact points and lines) (2).

Add the seam allowances, then draw a vertical line upwards from point I and point L, and remove any excess fabric (3).

Now we can close the seam of the sleeve (4).

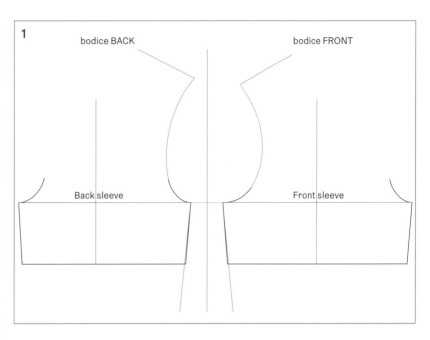

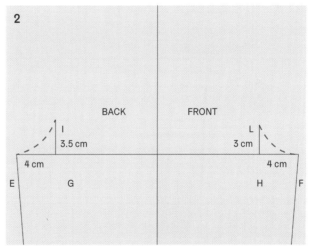

$E\text{-}G = 4\ cm\ G\text{-}I = 3.5\ cm\ H\text{-}F = 4\ cm\ H\text{-}L = 3\ cm$

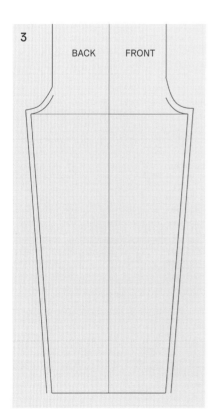

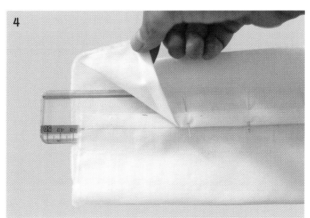

Thread the sleeve onto the arm of the dress stand.

Align the start of the sleeve hole with the start of the bodice armhole.

Choose the sleeve angle. In this case, being a classic jacket, the angle will be minimal.

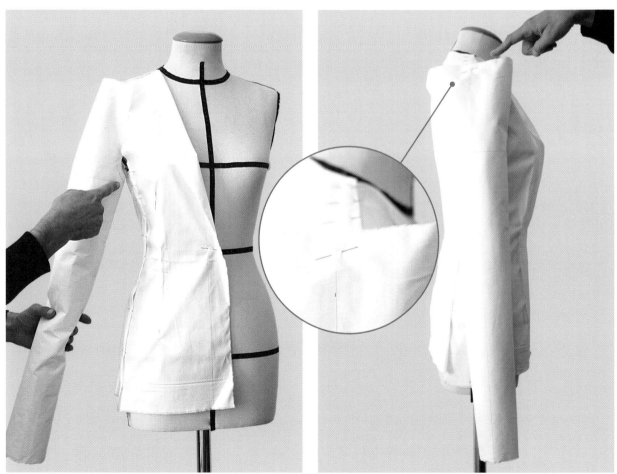

Use a pin to secure the start of the sleeve hole in alignment with the point of intersection between the side seam and the armhole of the bodice.

Use a pin to secure the upper part of the sleeve with the point of intersection between the shoulder seam and the armhole of the bodice, respecting its angle.

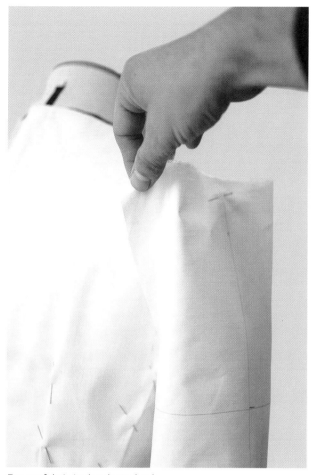

Excess fabric in the sleeve back corresponding to the back of the bodice.

Excess fabric in the sleeve front, corresponding to the chest front of the bodice.

Since this is a basic sleeve, you can remove the excess toile and leave 2 cm (0.78"), taking as a reference the clearance line of the bodice armhole.

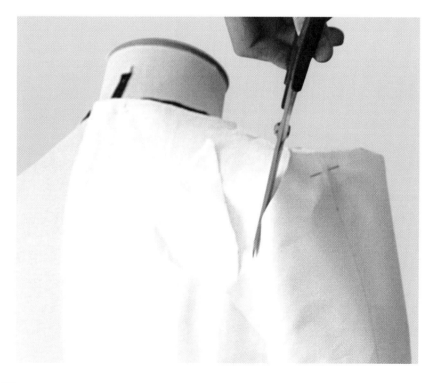

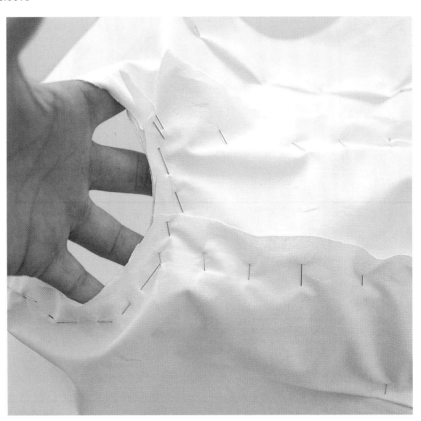

Now remove the model from the dress stand and secure the sleeve from the inside and the bodice in the lower part of the armhole.

Reposition the model on the dress stand and start to model the sleeve at the other points. Remember to fold back the toile in alignment with the previously marked bodice arm-hole. Secure the upper part.

Model the sleeve, trying to maintain the desired angle and fit.

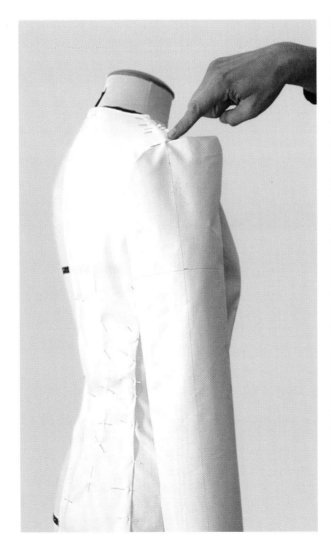

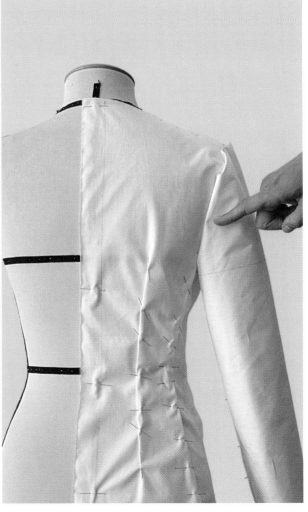

In the chest front and back, I recommend attaching the pins as if you were doing a hand finishing.

In the upper part of the armhole attach the pins perpendicular to the seam, maintaining the required yield of the toile in this area. This can change a lot depending on the fabric used (light, heavy, stiff, elastic, etc.) or the type of garment.

Once you have finished securing the sleeve in the desired position, shape and fit, you can perfect the length of the sleeve. Take a tape measure and mark the desired size.

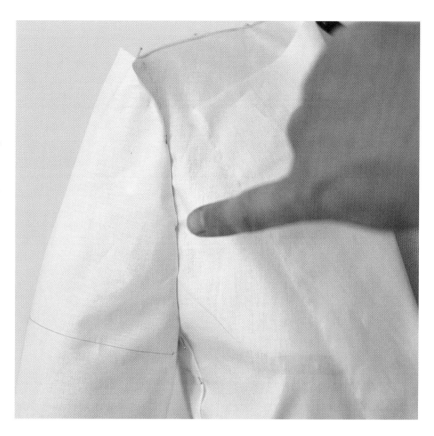

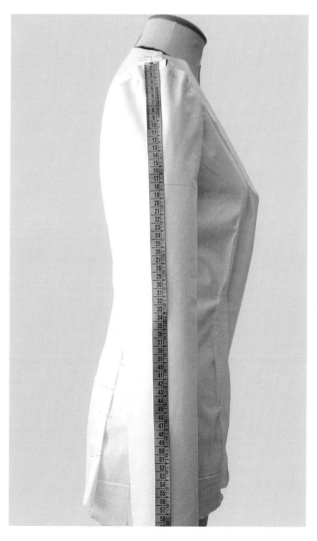

Control points of the model

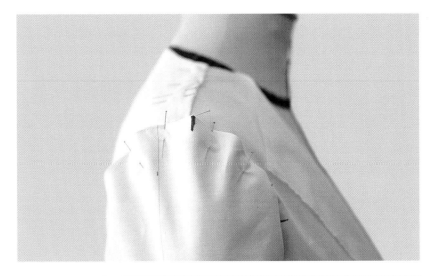

Now you can start marking the principal control points.
Mark the shoulder seam with a dotted line.

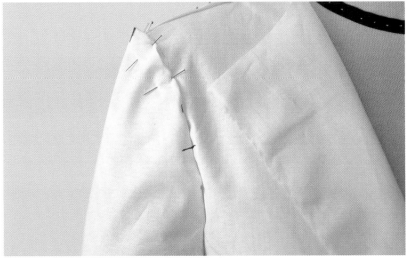

Mark the armhole front with a dotted line.

Mark the armhole back with two dotted lines.

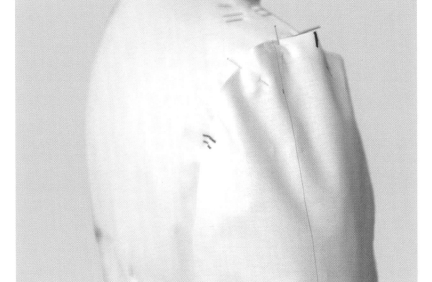

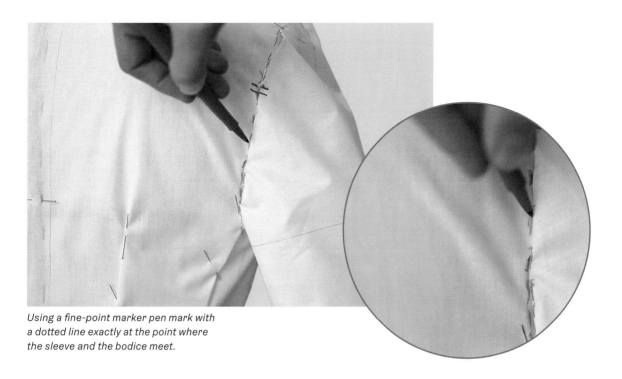

Using a fine-point marker pen mark with a dotted line exactly at the point where the sleeve and the bodice meet.

Remove the sleeve, lay it flat and with a French curve precisely adjust the cap-trumpet of the sleeve. Redraw the sleeve bottom including the hem.

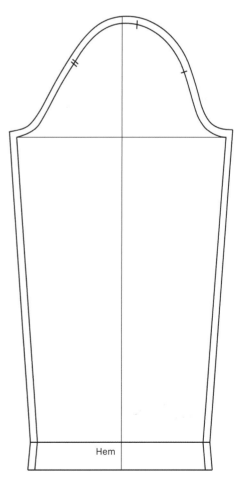

Hem

The basic sleeve of a classic jacket size 42 EU / 14 UK is ready to be put onto paper or digitised for Cad fashion software.

Raglan
sleeve

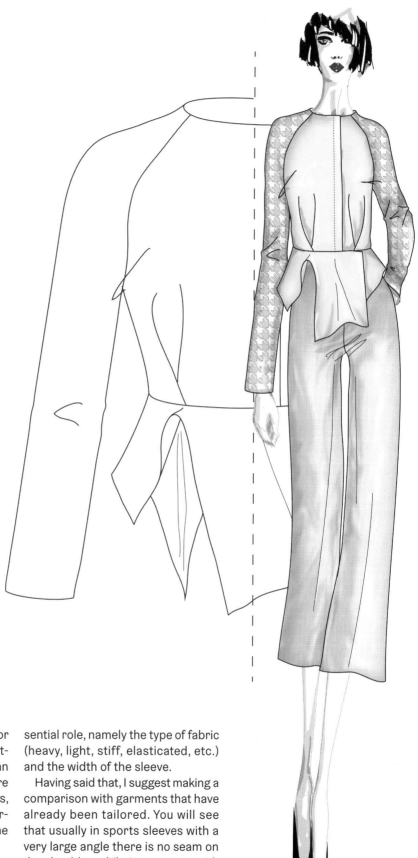

The raglan sleeve is usually used for casual sportswear, such as sweatshirts, t-shirts and jackets, but it can also be used for garments with a more classic fit. Think of MaxMara's coats, an important reference for this garment, reinvented over time since the 60s and often gracing catwalks.

What differentiates the sporty-casual raglan cut from the classic one is the fit. As already seen in the chapter on the basic sleeve, the angle is the first factor to take into account, followed by other ones that play an es-sential role, namely the type of fabric (heavy, light, stiff, elasticated, etc.) and the width of the sleeve.

Having said that, I suggest making a comparison with garments that have already been tailored. You will see that usually in sports sleeves with a very large angle there is no seam on the shoulder, while in garments with a smaller angle, a dart needs to be added in alignment with the shoulder seam which is of fundamental impor-tance in determining the right angle and to remove excess fabric.

Control points to be added

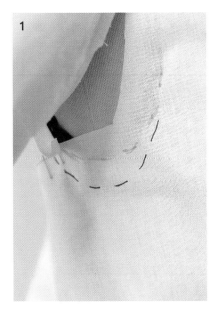

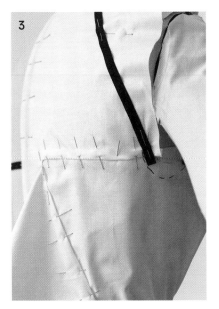

Reduce the standard reference of the dress stand armhole by 1.5 cm (0.59") and redraw the armhole (1).

Position the webbing on the front (2) and back (3) in alignment with the raglan cut and make it converge into the redrawn armhole at armpit level.

Where necessary, remove the toile outside the webbing references, leaving a couple of centimetres (4).

Take a black elastic band and position it at the same height as the armhole-armpit level of the bodice (5).

Remember that these references could change depending on the model to be made, so I prefer using an elastic band that can be shifted, removed and put back at any time.

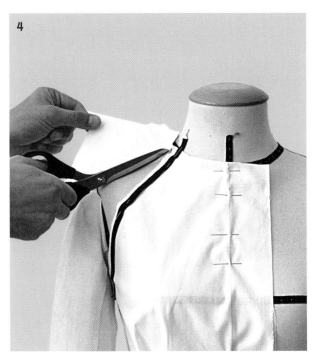

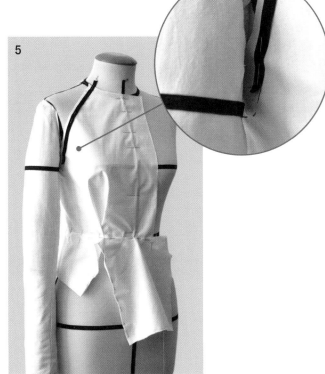

Preparation of the toile
to be modelled

Run the tape measure along the entire sleeve and record the measurements of the control points on the toile to construct the rectangle to be modelled. Proceed as for the basic sleeve.

The width of the sleeve will be equal to the width of the biceps plus the fit. Record the width of the bottom, give a shape to the cap-trumpet (which may change as you work) and copy the armhole front and back from the jacket base, or use the following rule.

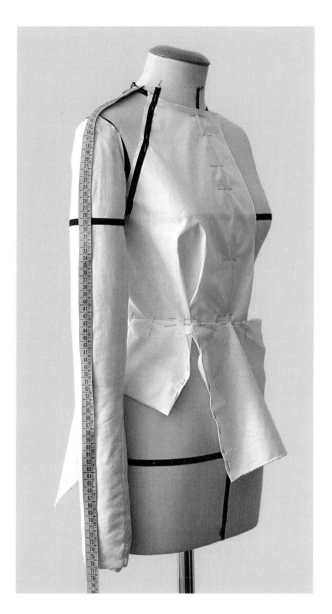

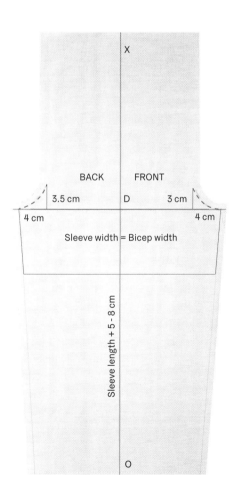

X-D = 29 cm (11.41") (length from the neckline to the armpit level detected on the arm). X-O = variable sleeve length (from neckline to the desired hem plus 5-8 cm (1.96-3.15")).

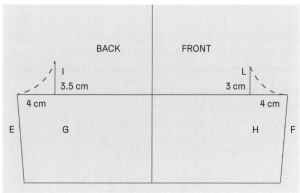

E-G = 4 cm G-I = 3.5 cm H-F = 4 cm H-L = 3 cm

183

Raglan sleeve

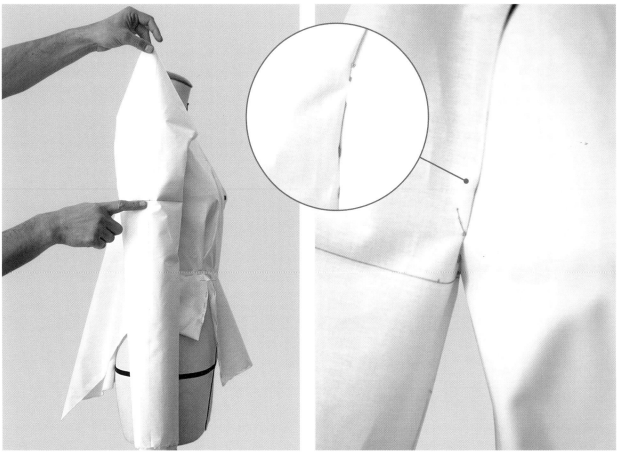

Thread the sleeve aligning point D of the
sleeve with the armpit level on the arm of
the dress stand.

Secure the sleeve to the bodice at the lower
part of the armhole with pins, attached as if
you were doing a hand finishing.

Decide on the angle by securing the toile
to the dress stand.

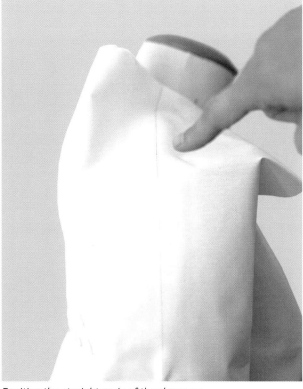

Position the straight grain of the sleeve on
the shoulder seam and check that it is true.

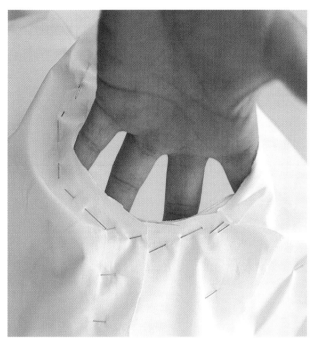

Before continuing, remove the model from the dress stand and, from the inside, secure the sleeve to the bodice with pins at the lower part of the armhole. If you need to remove the pins and position them in a different way to improve the grip between the sleeve and the bodice, do so: this technique lets you correct your work at any time.

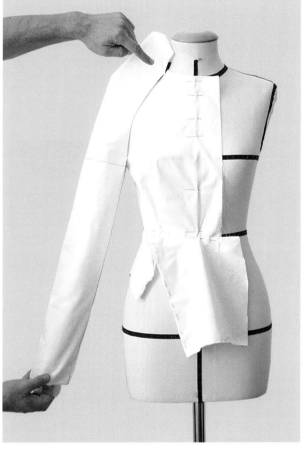

Put the model back on the dress stand and start to model the toile folding it back into the raglan cut, namely in alignment with the black webbing, and secure it with pins. Now there will be an excess of fabric due to the small angle of the sleeve. To remove the excess toile, add a dart or a cut-stitch.

Raglan sleeve

Cut along the line of the centre sleeve to the end of the shoulder.

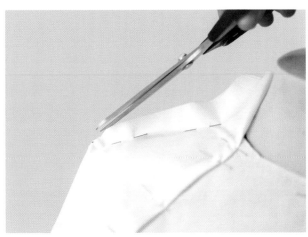

Temporarily join the two parts and remove the excess toile leaving a couple of centimetres and remove the pins.

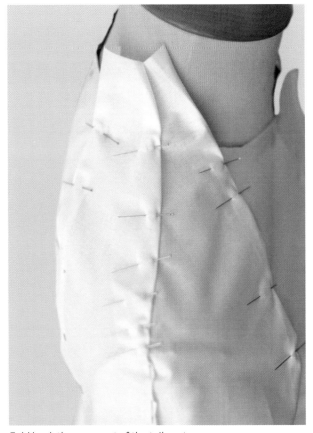

Fold back the rear part of the toile onto the front part, in line with the shoulder seam, and secure with pins.

Clean up the model and remove the excess toile.

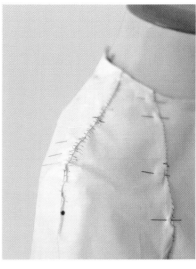

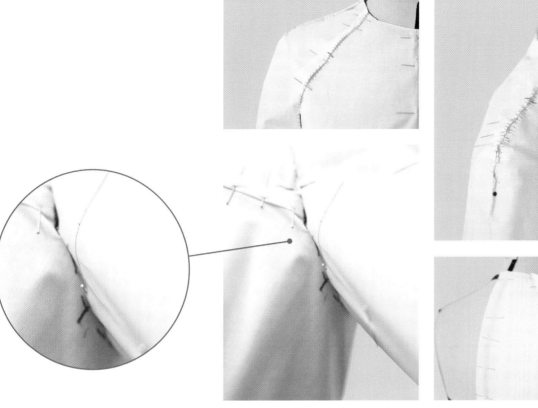

Detect and mark all the principal points, using dotted lines for the shoulder dart and for the front and back raglan cut. Where this cannot be done, use a red marker pen to draw a dotted line that marks both the sleeve and the bodice-jacket (armhole in alignment with armpit level). In this case the jacket does not have a side seam, so also make a notch on the bodice-jacket in alignment with the sleeve seam.

Disassemble the modelled sleeve, lay it flat and adjust the lines shown with a French curve. Finish off the entire model, including the seam allowances.

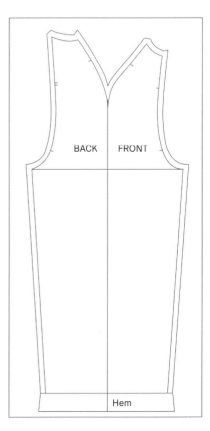

BACK   FRONT

Hem

With the raglan sleeve ends this book.
Now it's your turn!
Moulage is a technique without limits,
the only boundary is your creativity.
Just as a sculptor carves marble,
apparently without any rules but with a
rigorous and instinctive dexterity, the toile,
light as air and as fluid as water,
will guide you.

Danilo

PROMOPRESS FASHION COLLECTION

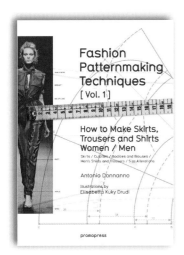

FASHION PATTERNMAKING TECHNIQUES [VOL. 1]
How to Make Skirts, Trousers and Shirts. Women / Men
Antonio Donnanno. Illustrations by Elisabetta Kuky Drudi

978-84-15967-09-5

210 x 297 mm. 256 pp.

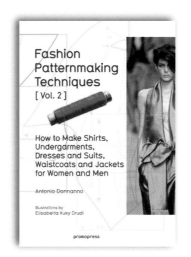

FASHION PATTERNMAKING TECHNIQUES [VOL. 2]
How to Make Shirts, Undergarments, Dresses and Suits, Waistcoats and Jackets for Women and Men
Antonio Donnanno. Illustrations by Elisabetta Kuky Drudi

978-84-15967-68-2

210 x 297 mm. 256 pp.

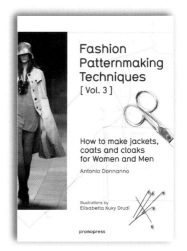

FASHION PATTERNMAKING TECHNIQUES [VOL. 3]
How to Make Jackets, Coats and Cloaks for Women and Men
Antonio Donnanno. Illustrations by Elisabetta Kuky Drudi

978-84-16504-18-3

210 x 297 mm. 176 pp.

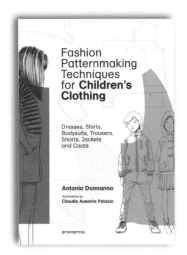

FASHION PATTERNMAKING TECHNIQUES FOR CHILDREN'S CLOTHING
Dresses, Shirts, Bodysuits, Trousers, Shorts, Jackets and Coats
Antonio Donnanno. Illustrations by Claudia Ausonia Palazio

978-84-16851-14-0

210 x 297 mm. 232 pp.

FASHION PATTERNMAKING TECHNIQUES HAUTE COUTURE [VOL. 1]
Haute Couture Models, Draping Techniques, Decorations
Antonio Donnanno

978-84-16504-66-4

210 x 297 mm. 256 pp.

FASHION PATTERNMAKING TECHNIQUES ACCESSORIES
Shoes, Bags, Hats, Gloves, Ties, Buttons. It Includes Clothing for Dogs
Antonio Donnanno

978-84-16851-61-4

210 x 297 mm. 240 pp.

COLOUR IN FASHION ILLUSTRATION
Drawing and Painting Techniques
Tiziana Paci

978-84-16851-59-1

215 x 287 mm. 320 pp.

FASHION ILLUSTRATION & DESIGN
Methods & Techniques for Achieving Professional Results
Manuela Brambatti

978-84-16851-06-5

215 x 300 mm. 240 pp.

PALETTE PERFECT
Color Combinations Inspired by Fashion, Art & Style
Lauren Wager

978-84-15967-90-3

148 x 210 mm. 304 pp.

FASHION DETAILS
4,000 Drawings
Elisabetta Kuky Drudi

978-84-92810-95-6

195 x 285 mm. 384 pp.

FASHION SKETCHING
Templates, Poses and Ideas for Fashion Design
Claudia Ausonia Palazio

978-84-16504-10-7

195 x 285 mm. 272 pp.

FASHION DRAWING COURSE
From Human Figure to Fashion Illustration
Juan Baeza

978-84-15967-06-4

210 x 297 mm. 208 pp.

KNITWEAR FASHION DESIGN
Drawing Knitted Fabrics and Garments
Maite Lafuente

978-84-16851-17-1

215 x 255 mm. 160 pp.

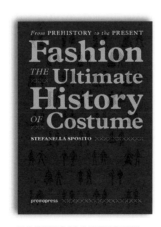

FASHION HISTORY
The Ultimate History of Costume from Prehistory to the Present
Stefanella Sposito

978-84-15967-82-8

195 x 275 mm. 256 pp.

FABRICS IN FASHION DESIGN
The Way Successful Fashion Designers Use Fabrics
Stefanella Sposito.
Photos by Gianni Pucci

978-84-16851-28-7

230 x 240 mm. 336 pp.